Craft
& Own
Your Career

Craft & Own Your Career

THE ZERO-FLUFF GUIDE

To Ignite Your Purpose
and Map Your Path

ROBERT CORBETT

THE
Corbett
GROUP

CRAFT AND OWN YOUR CAREER:
The Zero-Fluff Guide to Ignite Your Purpose and Map Your Path

Copyright ©2025 by Robert Corbett, published by Corbett Group, LLC

Contact the publisher at: bob@fullyaligned.com

First edition

Printed in the United States of America

ISBN: 979-8-9990488-0-6 (Paperback)

ISBN: 979-8-9990488-1-3 (Hard Cover)

ISBN: 979-8-9990488-2-0 (eBook)

Library of Congress Control Number: 2025912890

Editing by Deborah Ager, Radiant Media Labs, LLC, www.radiantmedialabs.com

Cover design and interior formatting by Becky's Graphic Design®, LLC www.BeckysGraphicDesign.com

Publisher's Cataloging-in-Publication Data

Names: Corbett, Robert D., author.

Title: Craft and own your career : the zero-fluff guide to ignite your purpose and map your path / Robert Corbett.

Description: Includes bibliographical references. | Corbett Group, LLC, 2025.

Identifiers: LCCN: 2025912890 | ISBN: 979-8-9990488-1-3 (hardcover)

Subjects: LCSH Career changes. | Career development. | Job satisfaction. | Self-actualization (Psychology) | BISAC BUSINESS & ECONOMICS / Career Advancement & Professional Development | BUSINESS & ECONOMICS / Personal Success | BUSINESS & ECONOMICS / Women in Business | SELF-HELP / Personal Growth / Success | PSYCHOLOGY / Career Counseling

Classification: LCC HF5384 .C67 2025 | DDC 650.14--dc23

To my mother, Dorothy, and father, Dee, for successfully launching me on this journey of life and for instilling in me the self-belief that with hard work and determination I could accomplish meaningful things and make a difference. I just wanted them to be proud of me and to know that their many sacrifices, encouragement, and sponsorship were well placed.

Like all parents, they wanted a life and career for me that was fulfilling and one of my choosing. Their message to me was that I was and had enough to develop the knowledge and skill to succeed; however, I had to be committed and willing to work for it.

Reflecting on my career journey, I'm proud to have a fulfilling career in leadership, coaching and consulting—as a leadership/executive coach and adjunct faculty member at Northwestern University, I'm doing the work I love. I'm helping others by giving back through my coaching and teaching—I couldn't be happier and I believe my parents are too.

Take the reins and experience the satisfaction, fulfillment and rewards from proactively and intentionally crafting and living the career and path of your choosing rather than a career chosen for you. Recognize that your path may not be linear and your career plan will evolve along with your knowledge and interests, allowing you to ultimately arrive at your desired career destination.

—ROBERT CORBETT

Contents

STEP 2

STEP 3

STEP 4

STEP 5

Acknowledgments

The messages in this book have been on my mind and clamoring to be shared for years: "Take the reins and experience the satisfaction, fulfillment and rewards from proactively and intentionally crafting and living the career and path of your choosing rather than a career chosen for you. Recognize that your path may not be linear and your career plan will evolve along with your knowledge and interests, allowing you to ultimately arrive at your desired career destination"

The ideas and messages shared in this book are a compendium of industry and organizational observations and personal and shared life experiences. The overarching message is the importance of taking a proactive vs. passive approach to achieving a rewarding career. Without the encouragement, expertise, and support of the people below, the messages above may never have been shared.

I thank my wife, Carmen, and daughter, Jessica, for energizing, encouraging and reminding me of the importance and value of sharing these key messages with others. Carmen encouraged me on days when I struggled crafting my ideas and messages for the book. Jessica gave me thoughtful feedback that she successfully used the process described here to confirm her career destination and develop and present her action plan to trusted advisors for feedback and support. She's also using the process to validate and explore her evolving entrepreneurial interests.

I am fortunate to have had and must acknowledge

the help and feedback of key individuals who challenged and/or affirmed my thinking and messaging: Rod Cotton, Eddie Turner, Laurel Delany, Jen Cohen, Perry Rhue, Ahmmad Brown, Debbie Plager, Stacy Gorin, Kelly Ross, and Charlie Baker.

I'm also deeply grateful to have benefited from the expert advice and guidance of my editor and coach, Deborah Ager, as well as the careful work of my proofreader, Vanessa Boeser, and my book designer, Becky Bayne. I owe the book's look, feel, clarity and flow to these three extraordinary professionals.

Brief Note to the Reader

"To bring about change, you must not be afraid to take the first step. We fail when we fail to try."

—ROSA PARKS

I crafted this book for those who recognize their own power and responsibility to continually envision, plan, commit, and follow through to actualize the career they want and deserve. This book resulted from me viewing my career journey from the perspectives of both a newbie and a seasoned professional to explore what I've learned about crafting a fulfilling career. Those lived journeys and experiences built the foundation of my OWN IT process, and I wrote this book to share my learnings and help others.

As a newbie, I learned the need to take personal responsibility for my life and career rather than expecting others to do that for me. Spoiler Alert: Along the way were times I put way too much trust in my organizations and leaders to determine my role and my career direction!

As a seasoned professional with a successful career, I learned the importance of being a reliable performer and of having trusted advocates to provide meaningful, important guidance and counsel. You can never have too many trusted advocates supporting you on your career journey. Success and satisfaction come by growing and sustaining these relationships. Looking back, I realized I could have been more proactive and intentional in planning and pursuing my career direction and leveraging my trusted advisors.

While the examples and stories I'll reference are from larger organizations, their ideas remain applicable for organizations of any size. Whether you work in a startup, small business, or nonprofit organization, you can benefit from my OWN IT process.

Along the way, I'll share lived experiences from my perspective as a person of color (POC). It's my hope that this book provides answers to any career journey questions you have along with a process to help you ensure you're planning and living the life and career you want and deserve!

—Bob Corbett, *Chicago, IL*

Asking for help from trusted advisors is a sign of strength, not a weakness.

CHAPTER 1

The Power of Owning Your Career

"The most common way people give up their
power is by thinking they don't have any."

—ALICE WALKER

Owning your career requires igniting change in your life by focusing your energy and attention in ways that help you creatively identify and pursue desired positive career outcomes. The *process* of owning your career includes taking back any power you may have given others to determine your career direction. Meanwhile, you choose what you want for yourself and take the actions necessary to make career progress happen.

As a new graduate, you may have said to yourself, "I'll pursue the best employment opportunities available and, once hired, demonstrate my value to the organization." You may have also thought some version of, *I trust the organization to identify the best role for me to leverage my education, gifts, and talents. Soon, I'll be on my way to a rewarding career, and the organization will know the best ways for me to contribute!*

However, as a seasoned and successful employee, you

may have found that you're not enjoying your current role or contributing in ways you believe you can. As a result, you may feel your contributions are not properly recognized. In both situations, you've delegated responsibility for your career direction to the organization. Taking ownership of your situation and leveraging trusted advocates will help you fix this. Making time and developing the discipline to identify and revisit your career wants on a regular basis help you end up where you want to be.

For a significant portion of my career, I was guilty of entrusting my career direction and development to the organizations where I worked. Initially, I focused on having a job title and pay level that my parents and peers would respect. Only after I'd weathered several unfulfilling job assignments did the idea dawn on me that I was part of my own problem. I hadn't identified my desired career direction or shared my career aspirations with decision-makers in the organization. How could they know what I wanted to do or be if I didn't know myself?

This reality led me to write this book and to share my OWN IT process, which I'll discuss in more detail throughout the book. The notion is that either you own your career or you're part of someone else's plan—and *they'll* own your career. Each of us has the ability and power to identify our desired career destination and the path to achieve that goal. Doing so requires a clear sense of Personal Purpose and personal ownership. Rather than leave your career to chance, you can exercise control by developing and executing a career plan aligned with your Personal Purpose and ideal career destination.

Owning your career is both a decision and action. No matter where you currently are on your career journey, it's never too late to **own your career!**

The Case for Owning Your Career

Career planning requires significant commitment, time, and effort. An unplanned approach to your career is like the theme of the 1989 movie, *Field of Dreams,* in which the main character hears a voice that tells him, "If you build it, he will come." This suggests that opportunities will come our way if we simply do the work, but that's not usually the case outside of Hollywood movies. You can be an accommodating worker and reliable person, yet you're not likely to go far without an envisioned destination.

The "no plan" approach requires little of you and says your career is like a leaf being blown by a breeze that will merely go where the wind carries it. With this passive approach, you'll wind up where you do by happenstance, which most likely won't be what you want. Questions to consider follow below.

- Do you want to leave your career to chance?
- What's the likelihood that your organization will have the same vested interest in your happiness, fulfillment, and growth as you?
- If your complete surrender leads to unhappiness,

unfulfillment, and lack of growth, do you have the right to complain?

Good news. An intentional, purposeful approach with detailed thoughts about your desired career destination will help you achieve success. The elements of my OWN IT process can help you accomplish the following.

- Identify your desired career direction and destination.
- Research career path options to reach your destination.
- Consider what will be required in terms of knowledge, skills, experiences, and capabilities.
- Choose trusted advocates who can help you.
- Decide on a timeline.
- Share and discuss the results of these efforts with your coaches, mentors, and sponsors for input on the reasonableness and fit of the destination you've identified.

Generally, my own early attempts at identifying my career path and destination were little more than a hazy dream of becoming a successful human resources executive and leader for a large organization. While I envisioned myself in a large office and walking the halls of the organization looking successful, I was leaving out a lot of details that needed to be clarified.

A hazy dream is not a plan—only an informal vision or wish. I had not even bothered to formalize my plan in writing, and research suggests writing goals down helps you achieve them (Matthews 2007). Back then, I believed that I only needed to develop effective working relationships with key leaders and successfully serve sufficient time with good and reliable performance in each of the human resources areas (recruitment, compensation and benefits, training, and development) and I'd have it made. I completely overlooked the importance of the key considerations I'll share in the following chapters.

Why Is Living the Life and the Career I Want Important?

Life is about choices, and you have the choice to live the life you want or to live the life you *don't* want. I believe you have the right and ability to identify and pursue opportunities that allow you to live the life and career of your choosing. That doesn't mean you won't experience challenges. However, you can choose to identify, ask, and answer the key timely questions that will provide the answers needed to plan and live your best life and career.

Your life and career should offer enjoyment, fulfillment, and opportunities to continually learn and grow. At a minimum, accomplishing this requires a sense of Personal Purpose. For the sake of this book, the term "Personal Purpose" refers to your purpose on the planet, what drives you, who and what is important to you, how you want to be remembered, and the other aspects outlined in the steps of the OWN IT process. You'll see I capitalize Personal Purpose throughout the book to remind us of this importance. The steps of the OWN IT process are listed in the chapter titles themselves and later in this chapter. Necessary elements include having a sense of your Personal Purpose and career direction. Ideally, the two align with each other. Before we go deeper there, let's touch on the mindset aspect.

How Do My Beliefs and Behaviors Impact My Career Choices?

Your career is yours to craft. We plan for most aspects of our lives, including what we'll wear and how we'll spend our time. However, some of us take a passive approach to our careers and simply hope a successful career will happen by itself. Beginning to own your career and life by letting go of unhelpful beliefs and behaviors will reenergize your life and career and put you on a positive trajectory. When you adopt and embrace proactive and intentional beliefs and behaviors, you open up positive possibilities.

Behavioral change involves letting go of certain unhelpful beliefs, such as the idea that asking for help is a sign of weakness, that self-promotion is a sign of arrogance, or that the only opportunities for career growth are the ones that are communicated or posted. You can encourage positive behavioral change in yourself by doing the following.

- Give yourself permission to reflect and live your purpose every day.
- Understand your organization's culture and ambiguity along with the political landscape and how best to navigate them.
- Be open and honest about your feelings, thoughts, and desires.
- Display a willingness to share who you are and what you stand for with advocates.

In the spirit of this section's topic, the following quotes emphasize the importance of being accountable in life. To have and live the life and career you want requires accountability for your actions and inactions, as well as the relationships you cultivate. The quotes below underscore the key messages of the preceding career lessons, including the importance of taking personal responsibility for your career and of identifying and aligning yourself with the right trusted advocates, including coaches, colleagues, mentors, and sponsors.

> "My life's purpose, direction, and accomplishments are my responsibility. I must be intentional and committed...I'm the master of my fate, I'm the captain of my soul."
>
> **—WILLIAM ERNEST HENLEY**

> "When people show you who they are, believe them the first time."
>
> **—MAYA ANGELOU**

Why Are Key Learnings Important for Having the Life and Career I Want?

If we're not learning, we're stagnating. If we're not learning, we're becoming obsolete and likely repeating the same mistakes with no insight as to why something works or not. Can you think of any conversations you've been a part of where someone expresses a point of view or approach that is dated, and it occurs to you that this person is stuck in time and either doesn't realize that's the case or doesn't care?

A case in point: A successful new business development and consulting partner with a major consulting firm was masterful at identifying, selling, and implementing effective tried and true solutions for client issues. The partner was invited to call on a major prospective client and followed his typically successful approach of meeting to understand the client's issue before quickly recommending his best solution. He believed that responsiveness was most important to a successful client relationship.

In this case, the prospective client was less interested in hearing about the partner's alternative solutions and more interested in developing a trusted advisor relationship with the partner rather than a transactional one. The prospective client believed that trust and in-depth knowledge of a client's business were key to identifying and agreeing upon the best solution to the client's business challenges. The partner continued to push for a quick fix to the client's apparent business issue and the resulting sales credit. After several unsuccessful solution-oriented follow-up conversations, the client decided to move on to another firm.

This scenario illustrates someone who believed that success would continue if they kept doing what had been successful in the past. This line of thinking ignores the fact that change is inevitable and that you'll need to be prepared to make adjustments to achieve your desired outcome. Holding to this past practice can indicate a fear of failure, laziness, or resistance to learning.

How the OWN IT Process Helps

OWN IT is a dynamic process to identify, plan, and pursue your desired career. Career success involves continuous learning and reflection that requires you to identify, plan, and pursue your career goals. That success requires personal investment, intentionality, and active ownership. Engaging in the following will help you.

- Learn from your successes *and* your disappointments.

- Realize that success requires the support of trusted advocates, including colleagues, coaches, mentors, and sponsors.

- Validate and leverage the right mind shifts, personal beliefs, and behaviors.

The Five Steps of the OWN IT Process

You'll see these steps listed as the chapter titles too. Certain chapters lead you through the steps one by one, so you understand exactly what to do.

- **Step #1: Own My Career to Wind Up Where I Want to Be.** Determine and pursue my career choice and become the "me" I choose to be.

- **Step #2: Be Who I Am More—Not Less.** Determine what I want and where I am headed. Frame my future and set my path.

- **Step #3: Decide Now Is the Time** to focus my efforts to identify my career goals. Develop and embrace my career plan daily.

- **Step #4: Identify My Trusted Advocates.** Share my goals with trusted colleagues, coaches, mentors, and sponsors, and ask for their insights and help.

- **Step #5: Take Action.** Live and work my plan. Commit to embrace and execute my plan every day.

"The only way to do great work is to love what you do."

STEVE JOBS

CHAPTER 2

Designing Your Personal Purpose to Have the Life and Career You Want

"In life, the first thing you must do is decide what you really want. Weigh the costs and the results. Are the results worthy of the costs? Then make up your mind completely and go after your goal with all your might."

—ALFRED A. MONTAPERT

The Main Concepts of a Personal Purpose

Considering life and career through the lens of purpose encourages a strategic versus short-term view and facilitates a more macro versus micro look at our life and career to ensure alignment and fit, satisfaction, and fulfilment. In his book, *The Power of Purpose*, Richard J. Leider shares that your Personal Purpose is the essence of who you are and why you're here. He writes that your purpose is a source of direction and energy. Through the lens of purpose, we're able to see ourselves and our future more clearly.

I've used the process of identifying a Personal Purpose for myself and with coaching clients over the years. I'll share the main concepts of the Personal Purpose here to give you the background. Later, I'll walk you through the steps, so you can craft your own.

- Self-reflection: You take time to consider whether your life is heading in a direction you like and, if not, determine what needs to change.

- Intention: You focus on determining specific goals and corresponding actions.

- Proactive: You take action to accomplish your desired outcomes.

- Accountability: This refers to accepting personal responsibility for what you achieve or fail to achieve.

- Curiosity: You have an interest and willingness to ask questions and grow.

- Intellectually Humble: You acknowledge what you do and don't know and will invest the time to learn more.

- Commitment: You dedicate yourself to accomplishing a chosen, desired outcome.

- Active Networking: You develop a large network of trusted advocates, including coaches, mentors, and sponsors for timely advice and counsel.

Throughout our lives, we make various plans—weekend activities and vacations, for example. Some of us even plan our meals. However, with our career, we may simply go with the flow. We know how we'd like our lives to turn out during the course of our career, but we choose to do more wishing and hoping than planning and executing. If that sounds like you, don't feel bad. I did the same thing early in my career and will tell you more about how you can embrace a better path than I originally did.

How Intentions Help You Create Your Personal Purpose

When I mention "intention," I mean making the time to reflect and identify what you want to accomplish. Intention is not a linear act. Identifying, planning, and pursuing your career is a dynamic process. Change will be an ongoing element that will require you to be intentional and agile along the way to achieve your career goals. Both anticipated and unanticipated challenges are likely to make achieving your goal difficult at times. However, being intentional means persevering, committing yourself, and taking purposeful action to achieve your goal.

My personal approach to intentionality is to make my thoughts come alive by considering my "Why, What, and How," which I discuss more in the next section. I have a conversation with myself by writing and speaking my goal out loud, discussing goals with trusted advocates, and calendarizing my intended next steps. Naturally, I take action. When you move through the process of stating your intention, writing it down, discussing it, and calendarizing it, the idea moves from thought to reality and compels me to act. You can read more about the science backing the importance of writing goals down, accountability, and commitment in chapter 7, step #5, "Take Action."

The "Why, What, and How" of Your Personal Purpose and Life's Vision

Your Personal Purpose and Life's Vision are interrelated. Your purpose is your "Why." Your Life's Vision is your "What," and the answers to the following questions provide important insight to possible action steps, such as "How" you might approach achieving your purpose and Life's Vision. Your "Why" describes the reason you live the way you do. Your "What" is the goal that enables your "Why."

Confirm your purpose and Life's Vision with the help of these additional questions.

1. What is my Life's Vision? What is the current direction of my personal life versus where I'd like my life to be headed?

2. What will be different when I'm on track to live my Life's Vision?

3. What is my level of self-management? What is my level of commitment to achieve my desired Life's Vision?

4. What will I need to do more of or differently to increase and sustain the level of commitment needed?

5. What are my supportive key relationships? What current relationships can best support me in achieving my Life's Vision?

6. What new relationships will I need to develop for additional support?

Overview of How to Clarify Your Purpose

Purpose reflects who you are as a person and influences what you will or won't agree to do. Your words and actions represent what's most important to you and confirms your purpose, which is your life's calling and what drives you. Your purpose demonstrates the direction you've chosen to live personally and professionally, indicates who you wish to become, and guides you in both good and challenging times. The way you *live* your purpose can be an indication of the change you'd like to see in the world. Your purpose will evolve as you learn and grow, so you shouldn't feel stuck forever by the choices you make today. Your views will change and your knowledge will grow as you gain more experience and knowledge.

Your purpose may influence your assumptions, behaviors, and actions, such as identifying opportunities, approaches, and steps aligned with that purpose. For example, your purpose will likely influence your social circle, job, and career direction. Challenging times may also influence your behaviors, actions, and job choices. For example, you may make an interim job choice out of the necessity to meet certain financial obligations like food and rent. Even in this scenario, look for worthwhile knowledge and experiences you can gain along the way. However, when challenging times have passed, you'll look for opportunities to realign with your purpose and career direction.

Your purpose should have a long-term, strategic influence on your behaviors, actions, and choices. Ideally, your life and career decisions should align with your purpose. As a result, the more in alignment you are with your career and life choices, the less drama and more harmony and joy there'll be in your life. The desired outcome you want will require intentionality.

To start, recognize that you deserve to have and live the life and career you want. Block time on your calendar at least annually to confirm your Personal Purpose and answer the following questions.

1. Who am I?

2. What do I stand for?

3. What values do I live by?

4. What do I want to accomplish in my lifetime and leave as my legacy?

5. How do I want others to experience me each and every moment of every day?

6. Consider various roles you play in your life. For each of these ask: What would I like to accomplish in my lifetime as part of my legacy?

7. List your unique strengths, competencies, gifts, and talents.

8. Consider what you want to be known for. Write at least 250 words about this without editing. Let the ideas flow.

9. Answer: Where am I headed, and is this the direction I want?

10. Answer: How intentional and committed am I to this career direction? If not, why not?

After reviewing your answers to the questions above, answer the following:

1. What do I need to do more of to better align with my Personal Purpose and career to have the life I want?

2. Who might help me think more deeply about my next steps?

Alignment between your purpose, life, and career is a critical element for being able to be true to who you are—where your behaviors and actions serve as observable confirmation for you and others. Life and career alignment with your Personal Purpose provides an energizing sense of peace and of being on a mission of personal significance.

Prepare Your Personal Balance Sheet

*A copy of this plan template is available
in the resources section.*

Your Personal Balance Sheet is an invaluable document that captures who you are and what's most important to you. You can use the sheet as a resource when preparing or updating your Living Career Action Plan and can update the document as conditions change. Once you've clarified your Personal Purpose, your completed Personal Balance Sheet will provide a profile and baseline of information when you prepare your Living Career Action Plan. The Personal Balance Sheet Template is in the resources section and contains key elements with instructions that, upon completion, will help inform your Living Career Action Plan. What follows are excerpts of the key elements found in the template.

The Parts of the Personal Balance Sheet

- Your Personal Purpose reflects the key drivers you identify.
- Your career vision statement helps you look strategically at the desired direction for your life.
- Your values alignment statement reflects the main

values you live by and their degree of positive or negative alignment with your purpose, Life's Vision, and current career direction.

- Your career experiences statement inventories key career experiences you've had to date and reminds you of them.

- Your key career accomplishments statement should capture your key accomplishments thus far in your various roles.

- Your key professional strengths statement should capture the capabilities and attributes that have helped you achieve your success so far.

- Your key development opportunities are your most critical development needs and can strengthen your potential for continued success in your career.

- Your key relationships include the important connections you value with influential members in your network.

- Your key career preferences rank your preferences when considering career opportunities.

- Your key career goals include the desired goals you identify.

- Your commitment to self-management is a statement of how committed you are on a scale of one to ten to do the personal work necessary to achieve the career you want.

Preparing a Personal Balance Sheet can be a helpful tool for establishing a baseline from which to confirm your career direction, plan, and path. Earlier in this chapter, you had the opportunity to respond to questions to help define your Personal Purpose and Personal Balance Sheet. Remember to review your Personal Purpose and Balance Sheet responses prior to preparing your Living Career Action Plan.

Career success is a journey of continuous learning and self-reflection that requires the relentless planning and pursuit of your goals along with acceptance that learning is a continuous process. You can learn from failures and successes, and you can expand your knowledge and experiences through them. In this way, learning becomes both a habit and an opportunity rather than a burden. In addition to your growth in knowledge and experience, being curious and open to continuous learning increases your visibility, value, and the ability to shape your career. All of that helps you to have the impact you want. This is the definition of a "growth mindset," which refers to viewing our skills and intelligence as aspects we can improve. With this mindset, we metaphorically view the mind as a muscle and believe that effort is the primary driver of success instead of innate talent (Dweck 2006).

Career success requires your personal investment of time, self-reflection, intentionality, commitment, and ownership. In this context, the term "personal investment" means making owning your career a priority. This calls for scheduling time each week for self-reflection on your life and career goals, actions, progress, and next steps. This process requires intentionality and commitment to hold your life and career direction high in importance. After all, if you can't commit, who else will? If you don't care enough, why should anyone else?

Being perceived by others as thoughtful, proactive, and planful for your desired career direction can enhance your internal and external marketability and position you in the eyes of decision-makers as a viable candidate for future roles aligned with your career goals.

What Are the Benefits and Typical Outcomes of Living the Career You Want?

At a minimum, living the life and career you want provides a high level of personal and career satisfaction, clarity and direction, and a sense of stability and predictability. Alternatively, not living the life and career you want will likely result in uncertainty and a low level of personal and career satisfaction.

Living the career you want requires a Living Career Action Plan to move from your current path to a more focused plan that moves you toward your preferred career path and direction. While a plan may not guarantee complete success in life, the lack of a plan leaves your future to chance.

Overview of Creating Your Living Career Action Plan

Developing a thoughtful action plan includes defining one to three priority goals and related actions to establish your career direction over the next three to four years instead of only focusing on the next individual job. This planning requires the identification of supportive, trusted advocates—such as coaches, colleagues, mentors, and sponsors—to help you achieve your goals. Next, you'll identify the main challenges you'll likely need to be prepared to navigate. Then, identify the metrics you'll use to measure your progress with your goals and actions. Finally, consider when you will start executing your goals and actions. The OWN IT process will help you clarify this.

The Main Parts of a Living Career Action Plan

*A copy of this plan template is available
in the resources section.*

This comprehensive action plan should include your top one to three main goals; your one to two key actions for each goal; one to three resources you'll need; one to three related challenges; one to three metrics to measure success; and your timeline with milestones.

The main elements include these.

- Your initial key goals identify what you want to do differently to move toward living the career you want.

- Your initial relevant actions will be used to achieve your goals.

- Your important resources most likely consist of the right trusted advocates with the right knowledge and experience or with the right influence to help put you on your path.

- Your critical challenges are what will make achieving your goal difficult.

- Your success metrics answer the questions:

- How will I know I've been successful?

  - What will success look like?

  - What will be different?

Finally, your timeline reflects when you'll start the pursuit and execution of your career plan. Your related milestones provide more detailed due dates for the elements of your plan.

Steps to Prepare Your Living Career Action Plan

1. To practice preparing an action plan, review the questions and your answers from the questions shared earlier in this chapter.

2. Identify your initial top three priority goals to live your Personal Purpose and Life's Vision.

3. Identify your one to three actions for your respective goals to make the progress you want.

4. Consider how you'll know when you're successful and when you'll begin to take action.

You'll want to keep the responses for your Personal Purpose and Personal Balance Sheet for reference when you prepare your Living Career Action Plan using the materials and resources from chapter six. As you go through this process, it's important to:

- Learn from your successes and disappointments.
- Realize that success requires the support of trusted advocates.
- Validate and leverage the right mind shifts, personal beliefs, and behaviors.

Examine Your Beliefs to See If They're Really Serving You

The men in my family passed along the belief that successful black men showed their competence and made their mark by figuring things out and accomplishing their goals on their own. According to them, asking for help was a sign of weakness. I initially accepted this belief. However, as a young black professional, I observed that my white counterparts, though competitors with each other, would huddle and share information.

I learned the long and hard way that no one person can know everything, especially in large organizations. Sharing information and collaborating with others has been proven critical for success. The moral of the story is to validate and modify beliefs and behaviors that you hold, especially when they're proven to be untrue or ineffective. I've told my millennial adult daughter that asking questions and asking for help is smart and not a sign of weakness. If you never ask a question, people assume you know what's needed and that you have access to the necessary resources for success. They'll hold you accountable for knowing and meeting their expectations even if you don't have the answers you want and need. So, if there's something you don't know or have that's needed to complete an assigned task, be sure to ask.

A successful career may not always be linear. Gaining the knowledge and capabilities you'll need for your long-term growth, development, and success may require several lateral moves along the way before achieving your ultimate desired career role.

How to Handle Misbeliefs

In the chapters that share the individual steps of the OWN IT process, I'll be sharing behaviors and beliefs to embrace along with those to leave behind. In order to handle any misbeliefs that arise for you, I suggest the following steps.

1. Spend time self-reflecting and making time to think and honestly assess your strengths, development needs, experiences, capabilities, and interests.

2. Ask what you'd like to be doing in three to four years. Consider what you'd like to be doing, what level of work you want to do, with whom you'd like to be working, and what authority you want to have.

3. Review your strengths, experiences, and capabilities. Ask what current strengths you could leverage more and what additional strengths, experiences, and capabilities you need in the meantime to qualify for that role.

4. Identify and explore the interim roles or assignments that could offer the opportunity to strengthen your candidacy. Assess your development needs or gaps and the actions necessary to shift them into strengths.

You have a good idea now of how to develop the plan. Let's move into each step of the OWN IT process, so you can begin to make this process work for you.

Own my career so I wind up where I want to be. Determine and pursue my career direction to become the me I choose to be.

CHAPTER 3

Own My Career

"If you don't design your own life plan, chances
are you'll fall into someone else's plan. And guess
what they have planned for you? Not much."

—JIM ROHN

Owning a career means taking personal responsibility for
determining a desired career direction and identifying a
preferred career path, personal competencies, resources, and
the necessary actions to pursue it. Success requires a mind
shift from convenient, part-time, and passive engagement
with a career to a proactive ownership.

My Big Mistake

My parents told me throughout my childhood that, as a POC,
I had to always be at my best to compete successfully with
my white counterparts. In other words, I had to be smart,
prepared, and at least two to three times better than others in
completing an assigned task. So, when I started my career, I
believed that working hard and demonstrating my knowledge
and capabilities would help me be successful at work. I also
believed that leadership knew the organization's strategic
direction and key roles, as well as the top talent available

within the organization. My assumption was that I'd be on the list of top candidates for upcoming key job opportunities when I performed well. After all, I thought the organization's leaders would know what was best for me.

What I didn't realize then was that I was looking for organizational leaders to determine what my next job move should be. Instead of taking ownership of my career, I was delegating the responsibility to define my own career plan to other people. In addition, I was entrusting them with the responsibility to define and satisfy my wants, needs, and passions. Since my work and personal lives were intertwined, I was also giving other people the responsibility for the quality of those lives. Therefore, I surrendered the right to complain about my career journey or where I might end up.

At the time, I didn't believe my responsibility included assessing my career passions, conducting the necessary organizational research, and creating the right network connections to help me identify, plan, and pursue the career direction I wanted.

As a POC in a predominately white work environment with no sense of psychological safety, I felt somewhat insecure and believed that I needed to keep my head down, maintain a low profile, and let my work performance speak for me. I wanted to be seen as a collaborative, high-energy team member focused on high-quality work contributions. I didn't want to be seen as a threat to my white colleagues. I strove to appear apolitical. While I maintained an awareness of the organizational politics that could impact me, I did not want to be seen as an active participant in those politics. This, I hoped, would give me time to establish my value and upside career potential in the organization.

Success requires letting go of certain ideas and beliefs

and replacing them with a new way of thinking. That's what I needed to do in my own case. When you subscribe to passive and erroneous beliefs or behaviors, you likely believe that passive involvement in pursuing your career goals is good enough for a successful career, and the organization will value you if you do good work. That's not quite how the career process works, and I learned that lesson.

The Hard Lesson I Learned

Early in my career, I participated in a management trainee program in manufacturing where we'd rotate assignments every six to twelve months. The objective was to give you exposure to various parts of the business while developing your organizational knowledge and leadership skills. Between my second and third rotations, I met with my sponsor in his office. He wore a blue cardigan sweater and was leaning back in his chair.

I took a seat. After exchanging pleasantries, I asked, "What's next for me?"

To my surprise, he leaned forward in his chair with his brows furrowed together. A cold tingle ran up my spine.

He replied, "What do you think should be next?"

I paused for a moment to think. "I'm not sure," I said. "I thought you'd tell me what should be next for me."

He leaned back and brought his fingertips together as he thought of his reply. Finally, he said, "Your career is your responsibility. If you've not given thought to your capabilities and what you want to do next, why should I?"

He was right.

The lesson I gained was this: If I didn't know where I wanted to go in my life and career, I'd likely wind up somewhere I didn't choose.

If you don't know where you want to go
in life and in your career, you might end
up somewhere you don't want to be.

As a first step, give yourself permission to move on from any beliefs and behaviors that haven't served you well. This is especially true when people you know and respect have suggested beliefs and behaviors as correct ones to rely upon. You may feel that you're disrespecting the advice and counsel of a respected advocate. The reality is that you'll continue to seek and use the advice of others. Sometimes, their counsel will bear positive fruits and sometimes not. You must always decide whether to continue to use the ideas, tweak them, or move on from them.

To move from negative to positive
beliefs and behaviors, ask yourself,
"What one to three actions can I take
to embrace positive, proactive, and
intentional beliefs and behaviors?"

Questions to Help You Determine Your Career Direction and Path

Identifying your career direction and confirming your career path is the difference between having a focused versus a meandering career. You can plan for a career with a focused direction, which includes your consideration of questions like:

- Where do you think you want to be?
- What do you want to be doing?
- Who do you want to be doing it with?
- Where do you want to be doing it?
- By when do you want to be doing it?
- Where am I now?
- What do I need to do more of or differently to get there?
- Who can help me?

Addressing these questions allows you to move forward with intentionality to initially define and confirm your career direction. This includes identifying your desired pathway to have and live the career you want. You'll know where you are currently and the goals, actions, passions, and commitment required to move from where you are now to where you want to be. In contrast, a meandering career is an unplanned, job-to-job based career.

Key Factors That Affect Success

Often overlooked critical considerations for defining your career direction, path, and plan include identifying and giving credence to what makes you who you are. Giving consideration to your likes, wants, needs, and passions drives and sustains you to do the demanding work necessary to stay the course.

A successful and comprehensive career plan needs to take into consideration key contributing factors that affect its effective execution. These factors include identifying:

- Your key resources and sources of support.
- Relevant key challenges you'll likely need to navigate.
- Your key success criteria and how you'll measure success.
- Your timeline for getting started with pursuing your goals.
- Milestones you'll use to stay on pace to make progress.

Prior to finalizing the goals and actions, you'll want to confirm your current personal strengths needed to move forward in your career. Additionally, you'll want to identify development opportunities to be addressed to move forward. Next, you'll want to research and identify your required action steps to eliminate your gaps.

Understanding what your organization values most—knowledge, competencies, relationships, behaviors, personal style, and performance expectations—enables you to assess the degree to which you have demonstrated or need to demonstrate more of what your organization values. This can help you prioritize or reprioritize the way you approach contributing to the organization's success. Understanding and navigating the organization's culture and political landscape will help you know which cultural elements need your attention versus awareness.

Remember: Knowing your strengths, interests, passions, and gaps, and what your organization values are key ingredients for identifying your career direction and path.

Checklist to Determine If You Could Use a Mindset Tune-Up

Review the list below to see if your mindset could benefit from a tune-up. Certain beliefs and mindsets will hold you back from accomplishing your goals, and these include believing that:

- My hard work and intelligence are enough to ensure the career success I want.
- The organization will offer me the ideal career if I perform at a high level.
- I'm not capable of determining my own career direction and destiny.
- I need to be agreeable and apolitical, and that's enough for success and gaining acceptance.

To succeed, you'll want to replace negative beliefs and behaviors with positive and supportive ones, such as those following.

What Are the Beliefs and Behaviors to Embrace?

When you subscribe to positive, proactive, and intentional beliefs and behaviors, you are more likely to inventory your key strengths and development gaps to help you confirm your career vision and direction; confirm your key wants, needs, and passions in planning your career; learn the organizational environment in terms of what's valued, so you can expand your organizational knowledge and close your knowledge gaps; assess your knowledge, skills, experience, capabilities, and gaps—along with actions needed to address your gaps.

To have the successful career you want, identify any passive, erroneous beliefs or behaviors you've held but that have turned out not to be true. Once identified, you'll want to learn from them and let go of them.

Personal Mantras for Owning Your Career

Consider adopting personal mantras for use as motivators. They can remind you what's important. You can create your own or use these sample mantras.

- "I deserve and owe it to myself to be the me I want to be and have the career I want!"
- "I owe it to myself to take control of my career."
- "I owe it to myself to trust my instincts, judgment, and experience, to pursue the career I want."
- "I owe it to myself to honor my knowledge, experiences, passions, and interests to intentionally pursue the career I want."

Key Elements to Owning Your Career

- Take personal responsibility for determining your desired career direction and the actions to pursue it with intentionality and commitment.
- Let go of negative, passive, erroneous beliefs and/or behaviors.
- Embrace and adopt positive, proactive, and intentional beliefs and/or behaviors.
- Know what your organization values most.
- Identify how best to leverage your strengths and address your development gaps.
- Identify and articulate your personal mantra(s).
- Identify the actions you're committed to do more of to embrace positive, proactive, and intentional beliefs or behaviors to own your career.

Be who I am more—not
less. Determine what I want
and where I am headed
by framing my future
and setting my path.

CHAPTER 4

Use the Strategy of "Be Who I Am More—Not Less"

"Your self-worth is determined by you. You don't have to depend on someone telling you who you are."

—BEYONCÉ

How Holding Back from Who I Was Affected My Career

During my career, I focused extensively on fitting in and not drawing undue attention to myself while performing my role. I doubted that the organizational culture provided sufficient psychological safety for me to risk sharing potentially unwelcome points of view at work.

Using the "Rule of Three" was one of many ways I tried to fit in. While I was a leader at a global manufacturing company in the 1980s to 1990s, a commonly held belief by POC was that no more than three POC should be seen congregating and openly engaging in spirited and/or animated conversations together. They feared retaliation because our white counterparts and colleagues might feel uncomfortable and wonder if we were publicly expressing our organizational concerns or our collective disappointments. According to the "Rule of Three," if an additional POC joined a conversation, increasing the discussion group's number to four people, then a previous participant would have to leave the discussion. The fact that we genuinely believed this was necessary indicated that we were more concerned about fitting in than openly sharing information as our counterparts regularly did. At that point, we didn't even feel comfortable simply enjoying each other's company. We didn't feel comfortable being more of who we were because the organization didn't offer a shared sense of psychological safety and belonging for us.

This belief affected how I showed up at work and the degree to which I held back and carefully calculated whether or not to share my points of view. In part, this was because I believed that there was less tolerance for my mistakes as a POC and any mistakes I made would be judged more harshly than identical mistakes made by my white counterparts. As a result, I held back on sharing my points of view in hindsight more than I should have.

Another experience of not fitting in as a POC and feeling dismissed by white counterparts is an experience known as the "plop." As a newer HR leader with a healthcare company and a participant in a human resources leadership meeting, I confidently suggested a solution for a process issue with which the twelve of us had been struggling. I expected challenging or clarifying questions from my colleagues. Dead silence followed. My comment "plopped" and wasn't acknowledged, as though I'd said nothing at all. The conversation moved to other topics. I assumed that my suggestion missed the point or was not worth a response. For the rest of the meeting, I held back from offering further thoughts for fear of being seen as a marginal contributor. Much to my surprise, later in the meeting, a colleague offered my same suggestion and received enthusiastic support! Needless to say, I felt dismissed and a lack of belonging.

These experiences resulted in me holding back and bringing less of who I am to work. The net effect was that I didn't think strategically about my career. Instead, I entrusted my career to the organization and hoped that the decisions of bosses and others would align with my career hopes. Despite my disappointment from the experiences of the "Rule of Three" and the "plop," I realized that it was my responsibility to be more of who I am in the organization because it's way too hard and unsatisfying to hold back, pretending to be someone I'm not, just to fit in.

The organization lost out by not accessing or leveraging my full inventory of knowledge, insights, skills, and capabilities due to a culture that wasn't as inclusive, psychologically safe, or welcoming as it could have been and that didn't generate more of a sense of belonging.

As I reflected on these disappointing experiences to determine the best course of action, I determined that my options included leaving the organization, withdrawing and holding back further, becoming more emotional and outspoken, or reframing and recasting these negative experiences as opportunities to explore positive and developmental courses of action. In my situation, these courses of action included gaining a better understanding of what knowledge, skills, and capabilities the organization valued most and identifying how best to bring and leverage the best of who I am to work. This allowed me to let go of my disappointments and move to a more positive, proactive, and intentional course of action to learn the organization and demonstrate my value and upside potential.

More specifically, I assessed my situation (including my portfolio of knowledge, skills, experiences, insights, innate gifts and talents) and determined which ones were most in demand by the organization. Next, I considered my desired outcome from leveraging my portfolio. Finally, I identified one or two key actions I would take to better demonstrate my value to the organization.

In hindsight, I should have sought advice and counsel from my trusted advocates on being myself at work and on how best to share my points of view, as well as how to respond when my shared points of view were ignored or dismissed in work meetings.

Remember: When you know your gifts and strengths, and honor what's important to you, you're more likely to make decisions that are good for you and your career.

Reveal More of Who You Are

Rather than feeling obliged to "code switch"—alter one's appearance, behavior, speech, and expression to fit in and gain acceptance by the surrounding dominant demographic—to fit in at work, give yourself permission to bring and reveal more of the real you every day. This means bringing all or, at the very least, more of who you are *with* you when you cross the threshold into your work world. Doing this will enable you to contribute from a position of inclusivity and belonging versus holding back from sharing your points of view and insights. By doing this, you'll free yourself to contribute meaningful points of view and insights while leveraging your key strengths. If you hold back from sharing your points of view and insights due to fear, then your bosses, colleagues, and peers may assume you have nothing to contribute. Such an incorrect assumption can affect their perception of you as a competent and reliable colleague. So, why not regularly let leadership see the full range of your knowledge, skills, and capabilities? If they're not interested in benefiting from your range of skills and abilities, you can decide whether to stay or leave. Additionally, leaning on your trusted advocates, including coaches, colleagues, mentors and sponsors, for guidance and counsel on being true to who you are can accelerate your ability to do this well.

Thinking in this way enables you to confidently visualize your future career more strategically as a pathway to a desired destination rather than as a succession of available jobs. Thinking strategically like this enables you to project your personal brand (who you are and what you offer and stand for) with more self-assurance. Don't be a prisoner of holding back to fit in. Give yourself permission to intentionally embrace and leverage the best of who you are.

Since gaining success requires letting go of negative, passive, and erroneous beliefs or behaviors and embracing positive, proactive, and intentional beliefs and/or behaviors, let's take a look at what those are in this context.

The Beliefs and Behaviors to Let Go

Letting go of beliefs and behaviors that don't serve you involves a mind shift. These include the following: assuming the organization has a wealth of career opportunities and that a good career path will materialize; believing the organization's career paths offer the desired career growth at the opportune time; assuming the right career direction will be made obvious; assuming I'll always know about desirable career opportunities; thinking I have plenty of time; believing that having attended the "right" college or university will give me a leg up on others.

People who subscribe to the passive and erroneous beliefs or behaviors likely say, think, or believe the following: "The organization knows what's best for me—who I am and what I need to successfully pursue and achieve my career goals in the organization. In the meantime, I'll be the 'me' that the organization wants and needs me to be." Other erroneous thoughts that may cross their mind include:

- "I have the right pedigree, such as educational institutions and personal networks, so I can't help but be successful."

- "The organization will tap me when the time is right for my next move up the ladder."

The Beliefs and Behaviors to Embrace

Having these types of beliefs and behaviors in your mind and day-to-day practice will serve you as you grow your career. These positive beliefs and behaviors include: reflecting on the job assignments I've had thus far and what I've learned and leveraged from each; considering the extent that my career wants, needs, and passions are currently being met;

identifying which of my strengths to leverage more and which of my development opportunities to address; accepting that there's no time like the present to confirm my career wants, needs, passions, and goals; believing and accepting that I must personally and intentionally invest time to develop a point of view of what's best for me.

Career opportunities are driven by company needs.

Additionally, those who subscribe to positive, proactive, and intentional beliefs or behaviors accept that "I must make the personal investment of knowing who I am and the direction I want for my career." Consequently, they reflect on their career path and experiences to date (including capabilities, successes, disappointments, and key learnings) to provide a clear baseline from which to consider their desired career direction going forward. They make sure to incorporate their key wants, needs, passions, and interests when determining their desired career direction and path and hold themselves accountable for purposefully and intentionally investing the necessary time to plan and pursue the desired career they want.

To begin to move from negative to positive beliefs or behaviors, ask yourself and note, "What one to three actions am I committed to do more of or differently to embrace positive, proactive, and intentional beliefs or behaviors to 'be who I am more–not less' at work?"

Using Personal Mantras as Motivators

Personal mantras can remind you of ways to bring more of yourself into your work. Create your own or use the applicable ones from this list.

- "I owe it to myself to identify the future I want and my path to get there."
- "I owe it to myself to not let disappointment keep me from bringing more of who I am at work."
- "I owe it to myself to regularly schedule time on my calendar to reflect on whether and how I'm being more of who I am at work."
- "I owe it to myself to ensure that, when leveraging my strengths, they reflect more of who I am."
- "When considering my career direction, I commit to being more of who I am throughout my career journey."

Own Your Career Takeaways: Giving Yourself Permission

Following the strategy of "Be Who I Am More—Not Less" requires you to proactively and intentionally give yourself permission to bring and reveal more of the real you at work. Don't be a prisoner of holding back to fit in. Instead, embrace and leverage the best of who you are. See below for ways you can do that.

- Let go of negative, passive, and erroneous beliefs or behaviors.

- Embrace positive, proactive, and intentional beliefs or behaviors.

- Know who you are, understand your gifts and strengths, and honor what's important to you.

- Calendarize time frequently to reflect on and confirm the degree to which (and how) you're being more of who you are at work.

- Seek advice and counsel from trusted advocates— coaches, colleagues, mentors, and sponsors—on bringing more of who you are to work.

- Identify actions you're committed to do more of or differently to embrace positive, proactive, and intentional beliefs or behaviors to "be who I am more—not less."

Now is the time. Focus my efforts to relentlessly identify my career goals. Develop and embrace my career plan daily like breathing.

CHAPTER 5

Decide Now Is the Time

*"Learn from the past, set vivid, detailed goals
for the future, and live in the only moment
of time over which you have control: now."*

—DENIS WAITLEY

My leadership and executive coach clients have shared that they became sidetracked from the career they'd envisioned and swept up in enjoyment of the trappings of a series of well-paying, high-visibility positions that offered a comfortable lifestyle with an unfulfilling career direction. They shared the frustration of feeling trapped and believing it's too late for a change.

Rod Cotton, a former c-suite executive at Roche, pointed out in an email conversation with me on October 21, 2024, that an individual may have many reasons for remaining in an existing organization or role that they find less than fulfilling. Those reasons might include financial factors, family concerns, or available impactful role alternatives. I'd add "considering your legacy" to his list. He points out that if you need to stay in your current organization or role for now, you can at least start to explore opportunities in your current organization. Doing so will address your development gaps, use your existing strengths, and provide opportunities for you to learn and grow.

Life is too short not to pursue the career that really calls to you and plays to your strengths, passions, and interests. It's never too late to move from an unfulfilling to a more fulfilling career. If you identify a career that excites you and you expand and develop the needed competencies, the money and lifestyle will follow. Even if you're already on your desired path, you'll still want to engage in continual self-reflection to assess whether your passions and interests are being met. Additionally, you'll want to reflect on and reconcile past, present, and prospective learnings and experiences, so you can adjust your career goals and direction as needed.

My Story: Deciding What to Do Next

At one point in my career, I was going back and forth in my mind on whether or not to attend a graduate school program in organization design and development and to complete executive coaching training and certification. This was such a frequent conversation for me with my wife that she asked, "What are you waiting for? Either do it or stop talking about it!" Nothing was stopping me beyond my own inertia. In your life, windows of opportunity will open and close. If the opportunity feels right, you'll want to be ready to step up before the window of opportunity closes. So, there's no time like the present to identify, plan, and pursue the career you want. Why wait?

This experience reminded me of the many good intentions I've had during the course of my career and the time I wasted failing to execute my plan while I "prepared." I didn't put myself first. I was too busy focusing on the short term and meeting the demands of my current role while not being intentional and committed enough to define, actively invest in, and pursue my future. I didn't create a formal career action plan, engage in meaningful self-promotion, or share my career interests and passions with the right people. By the way, I *did* complete my graduate degree in organization design and development and the executive coaching program too. My experience with choosing to pursue additional education reinforced the importance of intentionality and commitment and is one reason why I discuss these topics with clients and in this book today.

For a significant portion of my career, I focused on the position title, level of visibility and responsibility, compensation, and potential when I spotted job opportunities. I was guilty of delegating responsibility for my career to the organization where I worked instead of being proactive and intentional. Not until I was a human resources vice president for a successful and rapidly growing organization that was acquired by another—that brought in their own leadership team and replaced all of us in the c-suite—did I realize I needed to take more personal responsibility. This hard lesson taught me to be even more proactive and intentional about my career going forward and illustrates how we can learn from any experience—whether bad or good.

At that point in my career, I needed to decide whether to pursue another human resources leadership role or move in a different direction altogether. In 2006, I attended a four-day life planning course called "Life Forward" at the Hudson Institute of Coaching in Santa Barbara, CA. As a result of that experience, I developed my own personal life and career plans and have followed this approach ever since. Through that program, I did self-assessments in a number of areas, including my strengths, successes, failures, learnings, interests, and preferences in considering my career direction and destination. Later, I developed my own templates and the OWN IT process to help my clients.

As a result of my career planning efforts, I determined that leadership and executive coaching was my passion and calling. To learn more about that calling, I attended nine months of coach training and graduated as a certified coach in 2007 from the Hudson Institute of Coaching. Giving myself permission to put myself first, let go of the past, and do the planning work and execution helped me to pursue the future I wanted and deserved. Finally, I successfully launched my own independent leadership and executive coaching firm and haven't looked back.

You can do the same with your career. Subscribing to positive beliefs and behaviors is key. Putting off reflecting on whether your current career direction is what you want and instead, figuratively, kicking this can down the road to a later time is potentially a license to procrastinate and continue on an unfulfilling career journey. On the other hand, this could be an opportunity to confirm that you're on the right path and that no course correction is needed at this time. There's no time like the present to reflect and confirm you're headed in the right direction. Having the career you want requires self-reflection, proactivity, commitment, planning, intentionality, and execution. Notice how, in my own story, a situation many would label "bad" (the change of leadership resulting in them replacing all of the senior staff) led to a positive and successful career change due to my planning and intention.

The Right Mindset Helps You
Navigate Career Growth

Psychologist Carol Dweck noted in her book, *Mindset: The New Psychology of Success*, that people tend to have either a fixed mindset or a growth mindset when working toward goals. When we subscribe to the belief that we have a fixed mindset, we believe that we are born with a fixed quantity of intelligence and aptitude. As a result, we avoid challenges due to fear of a negative evaluation of our aptitudes that we think we can't change. We tend to see obstacles and negative feedback as confirmation of our perceived low aptitude. This way of thinking results in a low level of self-esteem and persistence.

Creating the life and career you want using a fixed mindset that relies only on what you know today will be challenging. You'll have an easier time if you engage in a growth mindset with the openness to be a curious and continuous learner who learns from both successes and failures.

When we subscribe to the belief that we have a growth mindset, we know that the intelligence and skills we're born with can be grown and developed. We seek challenges for learning and mastery, and we view obstacles and feedback as valuable inputs for our learning. Dweck points out that people with growth mindsets tend to have a high level of persistence (Dweck 2006). Such persistence is necessary to grow in our lives and careers.

In her TED talk, "The Power of Believing You Can Improve," Dweck discusses how we can improve our brain's ability to learn and solve problems. You can do the same with your career. In her talk, she asks a useful question that gives us ways to think about any problem that might be too hard for us to solve immediately. She asks, "Are you not smart enough to solve it...or have you just not solved it yet?" (Dweck 2014). I invite you to consider this question as you work through the OWN IT process.

From our successes, we learn what knowledge and actions we might draw from again in the future. While from our failures, we learn the thoughts and actions we might want to avoid next time. While failing is not something to be pursued, it's also not to be feared because it's an important opportunity for learning and growth.

> "You can't let your failures define you. You
> have to let your failures teach you."
>
> **—BARACK OBAMA**

Accepting Failure as a Way to Gain Wisdom

In *Failing Forward, Turning Mistakes Into Stepping Stones*, John C. Maxwell wrote: "If you spend time getting more comfortable with failure and are intentional in clarifying the role it plays in your life, you start to view it as a natural and necessary step on your way to success and not as something to fear."

Failures and mistakes are part of the learning process *if* you take the time to identify the assumptions you made and the actions you took that worked versus the ones that didn't—and why. This learning process allows you to expand your knowledge and capabilities and build self-confidence. Building self-confidence ensures that you'll define and use failures and mistakes as learning opportunities rather than allowing them to define you or stop you from taking action.

Developing Your Own Compass Through Reflection

After identifying key learnings from successes and failures, use these questions to reflect and confirm what's important to you, including your key wants, needs, preferences, and passions. Remember your personal life and career are not independent silos. They're interrelated. So, an action or decision in one is likely to affect the other in some meaningful way. Ideally, a consideration of your wants, needs, preferences, and passions for your career should be pressure tested for their impact on your personal and work lives to ensure compatibility for both. A lack of compatibility means you'll likely need to make reasonable compromises to avoid the resulting disruption and unhappiness in one or both. For example, not setting appropriate boundaries in your work life or career can have a significant negative impact at home. Consider these questions to develop your own compass.

- What are my key wants in my life versus my career today?
- What are my key needs in my life versus my career today?
- What are my key preferences in my life versus my career today?
- What are my key passions in my life versus my career today?

With your answers clarified, you can begin to set priorities and achieve what you want. You'll also want to consider how well your answers align with your Personal Purpose.

Through continuous learning, you can develop new and targeted strengths and competencies aligned with your Personal Purpose and career goals, which will evolve as you continue to experience, learn, and accomplish more. You should inventory your strengths and competencies annually to clarify them and so they are vivid and conscious elements of who you are and what you've achieved. That way, you can readily draw upon them when needed and even expand their use.

Capturing your purpose and career goals—including wants, needs, preferences, passions, and strengths—will give you a sense of direction and a compass that's aligned with your purpose and goals. This sense of alignment is a powerful tool allowing you to assess opportunities that arise during your career as a fit (or not) with your purpose and career direction.

Beliefs to Let Go

Knowing what beliefs and behaviors to keep or let go can raise our self-awareness and help you identify what to keep or toss so you can improve yourself as you move forward. The beliefs to let go include the following:

- thinking that just doing good work gives you enough visibility and the platform needed to secure the desired future;

- believing that presenting a positive image and being smart and articulate is enough to gain support;

- thinking that engaging in timely, thoughtful self-promotion is bragging and unwelcome or that leadership will tell me when it's time to make career decisions;

- believing no one needs to know the components of my career goals and action plan but me;
- believing I can accomplish the components of my plan without help;
- believing I'll pursue my plan when I have time.

Those who subscribe to passive or erroneous beliefs and/or behaviors may believe that doing great work alone is enough to receive the career opportunities that are best for me; rushing is unnecessary; I've got plenty of time to identify and pursue my career; simply projecting the right image will lead to a successful career. No self-promotion is necessary; helping to shepherd my career is my boss' role—my boss has my back.

Beliefs and Behaviors to Embrace

A growth mindset along with embracing positive beliefs and behaviors helps you grow and move in the direction you desire. Those who subscribe to positive, proactive, and intentional beliefs and behaviors believe: "I know myself, including my purpose, passions, wants, needs, and preferences, and I'm capable of determining my future." Successful organizations have a lot of smart, talented, and ambitious people. The competition is tough to be selected for key roles and to receive the opportunities to have a distinguished and successful career. In some organizations, the pace is fast. Desirable career opportunities come and go. So, having the right mindset, knowing your desired career direction, leveraging your strengths, and addressing development needs will all help you be prepared for the right opportunities.

These positive mindsets and behaviors include the following:

- reflecting continually on what I want so my career direction and interests are clear to me and I can articulate them clearly for myself and to others;

- knowing what career direction and paths ignite my energy and passions versus deplete me;

- telling leaders what I want so they can help me pursue the best career growth situations rather than hope they intuitively know what I'm thinking and want;

- identifying and pursuing career opportunities that are aligned with my purpose and goals and that offer continuous opportunities to grow and close my development gaps;

- actualizing my career direction by preparing and executing a formal Living Career Action Plan including goals, actions, resources, challenges, success criteria, and timeline with milestones for achieving my career goals;

- treating my plan as a living document that may change and require course corrections along the way;

- living my plan daily so people know I'm serious and committed.

Career Success Requires the Following

Pursuing the career direction and path you want requires focus, timeliness, and urgency as opposed to casualness and triviality. Key decision-makers need to know who you are, what you want, what you have to offer, and what you will bring to the table going forward. You certainly can't expect them to read your mind to know your career goals. You have to develop trusting relationships with supporters and decision-makers. You also have to engage in self-promotion by telling them your desired career direction and the value you bring to a prospective new role and to the larger organization. At the end of the day, it's your personal responsibility to define and pursue your career goals.

Those who succeed in achieving their career desires define their career direction and goals. When they share this with other people, those people can understand their passions and direction. That's part of the path of gaining assistance from advocates. Those who succeed also take the actions below.

- They capture their career goals and related actions in the form of a Living Career Action Plan document.

- They recognize that their career vision and goals may change over time as the result of a growth in knowledge and experience and, possibly, a shift in passions and preferences. This will require them to modify and energetically pursue their revised Living Career Action Plan.

- They identify the key resources and trusted advocates who can provide meaningful guidance and counsel.

Preparing your action plan is not an exercise that, once prepared, is put in a binder and archived on a shelf for posterity. Your plan is a living, leverageable tool to be referenced, modified as needed, executed, and lived daily. The preparation of your plan should be aligned with your

Personal Purpose and based in part on your assessment of your Personal Balance Sheet results including your strengths, development opportunities, passions, interests, and key network relationships.

The preparation of a meaningful career action plan requires quality time, focused effort, intentionality, and commitment. After all, you are envisioning your future career journey and destination and then identifying the strengths to leverage and the development gaps to close in preparation for successfully moving forward on your journey to your desired destination. Being a willing and continuous learner along your journey is critical for increasing your value and ability to contribute in the roles you hold along the way. Remaining open to exploring new learning opportunities in real time, as well as through formal training experiences, positions you for strong consideration and success in prospective, upcoming roles.

Remember:

- If you don't have a career plan, you'll likely become a part of someone else's plan.

- A successful career may not be linear. Sometimes it may make sense to move sideways to gain key knowledge and skills in order to move up.

- Your career plan is a living document that will likely evolve as you continue to learn and grow and as your interests and preferences change.

- Having a formal career plan allows you to evaluate and make an informed decision about your future career opportunities by looking at the degree to which they're aligned with your plan.

- Your plan can serve as a career compass and help

you assess the fit of new prospective opportunities with your desired career goals, direction, and path.

Personal Mantras to Decide Now Is the Time

Consider using these personal mantras to remind you to be proactive and intentional about staying in the moment while pursuing your career goals.

- "To have the career I want, I must treat my career goals as real-time commitments and live my career plan each and every day."
- "I must be sure to share my career interests and goals with the right people in the organization."
- "To effectively share my career interests and goals with others, I must be crystal clear on my why, what, and how of my desired career direction."
- "I must develop and execute a comprehensive Living Career Action Plan. In addition, I need to develop goals and actions that capture the key anticipated resource needs and challenges I'll face in executing my plan along with the key metrics and milestones I'll use to measure progress and success."

Own Your Career Takeaways

- Let go of the idea that I must navigate my career direction completely on my own.
- Recognize that having the support of trusted advocates helps me reach my goals.
- Believe I'm worthy of a successful, productive career that allows me to grow and develop

personally while adding a positive impact to the organization.

- Give myself permission to let go of my fears and believe I'm capable of determining my career direction and goals.

- Engage in the self-reflection and related work necessary to know my strengths, development needs, passions, and interests.

- Prepare a career action plan to achieve my desired career directions and goals.

- View my career goals as real-time commitments and live my career plan each day.

- Recognize that my career action plan is a living document that should grow with me and reflect my most current desired career direction and goals throughout my career journey.

- Remember that if I don't have a plan, I'll likely be a part of someone else's plan.

- Remember that achieving my desired career may warrant a lateral move before moving forward.

- Identify actions I'm committed to do more of (or differently) to embrace positive, proactive, and intentional beliefs and behaviors.

Identify my trusted advocates
and seek their counsel.
Share my goals with trusted
colleagues, coaches, mentors,
and sponsors and ask for
their insights and help.

CHAPTER 6

Identify My Trusted Advocates and Seek Their Counsel

"Know where you want to go and make
sure the right people know about it."

—MEREDITH MAHONEY

"Networking with integrity creates a greater
willingness of all parties to be part of a human
conduit to serve as energy and a resource to one
another. Sometimes you will give more than you
receive, and sometimes you will get back more
than you give. It's not about keeping score."

—CHRIS LONDON

You'll need the support of others to be successful personally
and at work. The same is true at the organizational level, so
you'll want to continue to build supportive relationships and
collaborate with others to accomplish your important goals.
As a professional looking to learn, grow, and contribute to
your organization's success and achieve your business and

career goals, you're challenged at the organizational level to successfully understand and navigate organizational culture—and the politics and power, structure, systems, processes and procedures, competing organizational interests and expectations. You have two good options.

1. You can choose to go it alone and attempt to understand and navigate these challenges on your own.

2. You can seek the advice and counsel of respected and knowledgeable people who "know how things work around here."

Successfully navigating these challenges will require identifying and building a network of trusting relationships with the right people. A strong trust-based and supportive network is critical for personal growth and career success in organizations.

Advocates are people who know you and who have a vested interest in your success. They can be bosses or colleagues who value the relationship and want you to be successful. They are people whose thoughts, opinions, and/or feedback you value and may seek from time to time. In addition to colleagues, your network of trusted advocates should include coaches, mentors, and sponsors.

The Four Types of Advocates and How They Help

Advocates are trusted advisors who provide advice, counsel, and critical feedback. They are willing to publicly support you and to speak on your behalf.

1. **Coaches** are certified professionals who, in strict

confidence, help you focus on identifying and proactively pursuing your most important priority goals. For example, a coach may help you more effectively leverage your knowledge and capabilities, address individual development needs, navigate organizational politics, and develop and/or expand key leadership skills and relationships.

2. **Colleagues** are trusted coworkers whose point of view, feedback, and/or input you seek from time to time and find insightful and valuable.

3. **Mentors** are seasoned, knowledgeable resources and helpful in your current role. They know the organization's structure, political landscape, culture, and key roles. While they can be decision-makers, they're more typically influencers who know what it takes to be successful in key organizational roles. They may also be connected with relevant key decision-makers, including their selection criteria and mentoring capabilities.

4. **Sponsors** are typically senior leaders and decision-makers, c-suite executives, or those reporting to the c-suite. They're responsible for significant and critical functions for domestic and/or international operations. In addition to mentoring, they operate at high levels in the organization and are likely making key organizational decisions affecting career opportunities. Sponsors can play a significant role in introducing you as a candidate for roles that are aligned with your career plan and goals. These are trust-based relationships that are usually reciprocal. For example, you help your sponsor accomplish key goals. In return, they could help you

expand your network of sponsors and help position you to achieve your career goals.

To successfully identify sponsors requires a mind shift from going it alone to engaging the help of others and developing trusting relationships with them.

Checklist: Beliefs to Let Go

Knowing what beliefs and behaviors to keep or let go can raise your self-awareness and help you identify what to keep or toss so you can improve yourself as you move forward. Here's a list of what beliefs to let go.

- Belief to Let Go 1: If I appear focused or self-assured or am willing to share my point of view or ask for what I want, I'll appear arrogant, pushy, or not a team player.

- Belief to Let Go 2: I'm on my own career-wise because I'm not sure anyone's willing to invest in me and stay the course as mentors and/ or sponsors.

- Belief to Let Go 3: My colleagues, coaches, mentors, and sponsors won't take the time to get to know me personally to understand who I am or be willing to support me.

Checklist: Beliefs and Behaviors to Embrace

When working with your advocates, these behaviors are ones to embrace.

- Believing I can demonstrate my organizational value and deepen my mentor and sponsor relationships by continually and constructively stepping up to share my point of view;

- being willing to be vulnerable and to engage in responsible self-promotion by sharing who I am, what I stand for, and my desired career direction with mentors and sponsors;

- growing and sustaining my network of coaches, colleagues, mentors, and sponsors by deepening trust and reciprocating support by offering to help them achieve their key goals;

- sharing and asking for advice and counsel on my career goals, action plan, and progress from my coaches, colleagues, mentors, and sponsors;

- asking my mentors and sponsors for insights and guidance on strategies and tactics to achieve my career goals and plan.

Checklist: Beliefs and Behaviors That May Prevent You from Identifying Your Sponsors

The beliefs listed below are based on the perception that the keys to success are to be a top performer but otherwise maintain a low profile. The assumption here is that if, like my counterparts, I confidently and proactively share my accomplishments and career expectations, I'll be perceived as not being appreciative enough of my current role. However, when my counterparts engage in the same behavior, they're seen as confident, successful, and justifiably ambitious.

Without further ado, these beliefs and behaviors include believing the following.

- I don't need responsible and proactive self-promotion for success.

- I'm on my own pursuing my career, and I'll be considered arrogant if I engage in responsible self-promotion.

- I'm not likely to have the access, trust, commitment, and quality of advice and counsel that my counterparts receive from their mentors and sponsors for me to be successful.

The list above speaks in part to the importance of identifying and building trusting relationships with coaches, colleagues, mentors, and sponsors to help you successfully navigate the complexities of an organization's culture, politics, and structure. The reality is that it's tough to solicit the help you want and need if prospective mentors and sponsors don't know you or your accomplishments, capabilities, and aspirations. With this knowledge, mentors and sponsors can help you consider an appropriate career path and opportunities and exercise influence on your behalf with appropriate decision-makers. Without the support of supportive coaches, colleagues, mentors, and sponsors (advocates), it'll be you against a cast of thousands of counterparts pursuing your respective career goals, and you can bet they'll be supported by their own advocates. So, don't be disadvantaged. If you haven't already, identify and build your own portfolio of advocates. If you already have your portfolio of trusted coaches, colleagues, mentors, and sponsors, consider expanding your portfolio—there's no such thing as having too many.

Checklist: Beliefs of People Who Embrace Positive Beliefs and Behaviors

- Being willing to be vulnerable and ask for advice and counsel is not a sign of weakness and is essential to career success;
- expanding my network of coaches, colleagues, mentors, and sponsors is essential to ensure I have the depth and breadth of resources needed to provide the insights, access, and support needed to successfully pursue and achieve my career goals;
- believing vulnerability and responsible self-promotion is a sign of self-confidence and career ownership and accountability;
- achieving my career goals is more likely with the support of supportive coaches, colleagues, mentors, and sponsors.

Seeking and embracing these intentional beliefs and behaviors results in receiving meaningful advice, counsel, and help reading between the lines, interpreting situations, navigating an organization's challenges, and benefiting from a sponsor's personal political capital when they use their reputation, status, followers, and influence on your behalf.

Three Pillars of Crafting Your Supportive Network

The Importance of a Supportive Network

Having a supportive network of coaches, colleagues, mentors, and sponsors is essential. Otherwise, your personal mission will be to find a way to learn and know everything they know and have experienced all on your own. If this was easy, you could become a leader by osmosis and a network would be unnecessary. This sounds like mission impossible, especially considering that knowledge and experiences are continually changing to meet the demands of a complex and dynamic, rather than static, global world of business. So, that's all the more reason to identify, nurture, sustain, and have access to the personalized advice and counsel of your own personal network and portfolio of coaches, colleagues, mentors, and sponsors with whom to collaborate, plan, and pursue your career goals and destination.

Overcoming Discomfort and Putting Yourself Out There

Overcoming the discomfort of putting yourself out there and feeling vulnerable is a critical first step in asking for help without feeling it's a sign of weakness. Traditional views of value and strength in organizations include a need to be perceived as the smartest person in the room, all-knowing, able to answer all questions, and having a real-time solution to every problem. Today's global business complexity and technological advancements make the idea of any one person being all-knowing both exhausting and impossible. So, the logical solution is to be willing to collaborate with others to accomplish what's important to you. This recognition is a sign of maturity, strength, and commitment both to the organization and personal success.

Identify a Personal Board of Directors

After identifying, expanding, and sustaining your supportive network of coaches, colleagues, mentors, and sponsors, identify your Personal Board of Directors (PBOD) consisting of select mentors and sponsors in your network that you value and trust the most. The idea is to find those people who can provide guidance and counsel on your most important plans and decisions. Consider the mentors and sponsors who've provided the most timely and beneficial advice and counsel so far and then discuss with them their willingness to be members of your PBOD. Be sure to discuss their key goals and how you could be of help to them.

How Adopting a Networking Profile Helps You Establish Meaningful Connections with Advocates

I've emphasized the importance of establishing a strong network of trusted advocates. Gaining knowledge of common networking "types" can help you assess the networker you are and want to become while improving your outcomes. John Philbin, career coach and co-founder of Happy Spectacular Life, discusses four types of networkers in an article on his website. He writes that "a healthy career is a connected career and it's never too late to start to build a network that works."

I believe that three of the four types Philbin lists are the most productive ones, so I'm describing three of them here and leaving out the fourth one he calls "Weak and Disconnected." Considering the adoption of these three types of networker profiles will help you the most, especially when developing your trusted advocate relationships.

1. A **"Big and Broad"** networking approach identifies you as a connector, who is always looking to make connections. You see who else within your network "needs" to meet each other while also connecting

on your own behalf. The disadvantage to this type is you can easily be pulled in too many directions while trying to help so many other people.

2. A **"Narrow and Focused"** networker already knows enough people. This type selectively attends events after determining if the return on investment will be worth the time. The disadvantage? This networking type can become stale.

3. A **"Strategic and Proactive"** networker uses their existing connections to get a meeting. This type aims for specific connections by creating a plan. The challenge with this type is that you have to ensure that establishing the relationship is valuable for the other person so as not to be viewed as merely a user.

During my career as a corporate human resources leader, I tended to use the "Narrow and Focused" and "Strategic and Proactive" approaches to networking in order to incorporate the right people in my network. However, as a leadership and executive coach, my focus shifted. To expand my own networking approach, I've included "Big and Broad" to be a connector helping others expand their networks while expanding my own at the same time. Notice how my addition to my networking approach illustrates the idea of continuous learning that I talk about throughout the book. No matter what stage of our career or lives we might be in, we have the ability to learn and change our ways. To start, experiment with one approach and reflect on how well that works. You can always change your approach to suit your career stage, preferences, and goals.

Networking Tip:

You can track your outreach in a spreadsheet, so you can stay on top of your outreach and ensure you're reaching out to people on a regular basis. Doing this will benefit you and your network over the long term.

My Story: How Networking Helped Me Accomplish Priorities

In my role as the new director of global compensation and benefits for a global manufacturing company, I made executive compensation program recommendations to the compensation committee of the board of directors. I made it a point to introduce myself and develop trusting relationships with the committee members. After getting the approval of company leadership for our compensation recommendations, I also made it a point to share and pre-sell the key elements of my planned compensation recommendations with committee members to ensure there were no surprises. On one occasion, a key committee member alerted me that another influential member would have a significant concern about our recommendations. The key committee member took the time to alert me due to the relationship we'd built over time. This enabled me to tweak my recommendations before meeting with that committee member and avoid a significant embarrassing misstep for me and company leadership with the compensation committee.

As the director of human resources for the headquarters location of a global health services company, I developed a broad network that included senior leadership. Along the way, a senior leader and trusted member of my network decided to leave the organization to join a global manufacturing organization as their CEO and invited me to join him as his vice president of human resources. I accepted the offer. This is only one example of how creating and maintaining a trusted network can be beneficial.

Identify Networking Competencies to Build Your Career

In addition to being knowledgeable about common networking types, knowing the key competencies for successful networking can help you craft your career. Vern Schellenger, president and CEO of Contacts Count details eight key networking competencies.

1. **Adopt a Positive Networking Identity**: To create mutually beneficial relationships, project a positive networker identity.

2. **Take a Strategic Approach**: Align your networking conversations with your goals, projects, and interests so you enjoy the experience.

3. **Develop Trust-Based Relationships**: While networking and building relationships, take time to learn about each other's character, interests, and abilities. Trust can begin with shared interests, such as running marathons or enjoying the same

musicians. Not every moment of discussion has to be about work.

4. **Engage Others**: For rich conversations, ask engaging questions, actively listen, and learn about your conversation partner's interests and abilities. Be sure to take notes so you recall what they said.

5. **Network Gracefully**: Be confident, likeable, and professional. Strengthen relationship bonds by being attentive to relationship-building rituals, including following up, being present and attentive, and prioritizing the relationship.

6. **Envision Your Ideal Network**: Identify your ideal network. This could include people from work or elsewhere.

7. **Communicate Your Expertise**: Mentioning your expertise is okay. Just be sure you don't spend ten minutes straight talking about yourself. Be sure you're allowing the other person to speak too. If we become nervous, it's easy to start talking too much.

8. **Achieve More and Give More**: Network to contribute to your success and the success of others.

During the human resources leadership segment of my career, I focused on doing work responsively and well. As the director of compensation and benefits for an aerospace company, I was a newbie to the industry and relied on building strong relationships through effective networking. Networking was essential for me to comprehend the organizational context and to navigate and provide the right compensation and benefits services for both the public and secret segments of the business. My job was partly to ensure that both leaders and teams could access and use the organization's salary, rewards, and benefits programs. I scheduled reciprocal one-on-one leader meetings across operations to introduce myself, learn about their segment of the business, and understand their needs.

Over months, I attended and took advantage of company sponsored meetings to introduce myself and learn the roles and needs of colleagues across business operations. Needless to say, networking expedited the pace and comprehensiveness of my growth in knowledge and experience.

In my networking efforts in that position, I focused on following six competencies projecting a positive networking image:

1. aligning networking conversations with mutual goals and interests;

2. developing trust-based relationships;

3. listening and asking engaging, thought-provoking questions;

4. being confident, likeable, and professional;

5. developing and sustaining a large, strong, and diverse network;

6. engaging in a reasonable amount of self-promotion.

Ways to Build Trust

A centerpiece for developing deep, reciprocal relationships is trust. In trusting relationships, you have a vested interest in each other's success, keep each other's best interests in mind, and give each other the benefit of the doubt.

The FranklinCovey blog shared behaviors that facilitate building high-trust relationships. While I believe they're all important, the selection of behaviors noted below have been especially important in my efforts to develop and sustain productive and trust-based relationships. The first behavior, "Talk Straight," sets the tone for building trusting relationships because a listener trusts you more if your delivery is direct and clearly articulated. In other words, no one wants to be forced to "read between the lines" to understand you.

The following includes the definitions for the behaviors I'm addressing here.

- **Talk Straight**: Be clear in your communication, letting others know your intent. Avoid insincere flattery, deception, misinformation, spin, and manipulation.

- **Demonstrate Respect**: Be respectful, showing fairness, kindness, and civility to all—not just those you believe can help you.

- **Clarify Expectations**: Establish and agree on a clear shared vision and agreed-upon expectations.

- **Deliver Results**: Meet your commitments by delivering what you promise on time and in a way that's consistent with expectations.

- **Get Better**: Don't stand pat. Continue to learn, grow, and develop. Seek feedback. When mistakes are made, learn from them.

- **Practice Accountability**: Be accountable along with others for agreed-upon outcomes and their timely communication.

- **Keep Commitments**: Do what you say when you said you were going to do it. This is the quickest way to build trust.

- **Extend Trust**: This helps to build reciprocity in

relationships. So, extend it conditionally to those who are earning your trust and abundantly to those who've already earned it.

Key behaviors in trust-based relationships are transparent and respectful conversations, listening to understand and being influenced by what's discussed, defining clear expectations for the relationship, keeping commitments, and knowing that it's possible that trust may be extended before being earned.

Who Should You Include in Your Network?

I've emphasized the importance of having trusted advocates in your network, including coaches, colleagues, mentors, and sponsors. Rachel Wells, in an article published in *Forbes*, indicates additional types of people to include:

- **Industry Peer(s)**: Professional connections with whom you can exchange best practices in navigating organizational challenges and who open opportunities for collaboration and strategic partnership. Industry peers can be colleagues who are internal or external to your organization.

- **Industry Thought Leader(s)**: Individuals who've built an extensive personal brand are respected and trusted by peers whose knowledge, insights, and perspectives on trends, policies, and ideas you'll want to regularly access. This could potentially help position you as an upcoming thought leader. Industry thought leaders can be sponsors who are internal or external to your organization.

- **Emerging Talent**: Individuals who are newer to

the profession. Become a more effective leader of diverse teams and challenge old ways of thinking by keeping your leadership skills fresh and agile by engaging with emerging young talent and valuing their diverse perspectives and ways of thinking. Emerging talent includes team members you lead and develop. You may even mentor or sponsor them one day.

To start finding the right people for your network, identify prospective members already in your world that fit these types. Second, identify prospective members who will fill types currently missing from your network. Third, begin engaging with them. Remember to identify current or prospective internal and external advocates who, by virtue of a large and positive reputation, could be your sponsors.

How to Leverage Your Networking Opportunities

To this day, developing trusting and supportive relationships with sponsors has been extremely important because they are advocates—individuals who are, or have been, in a position to influence a favorable career or business outcome due to their organizational level, authority, reputation, influence, and political capital. So, how do I develop a trusting, productive relationship with sponsors?

My goal is to develop and sustain long-term, trust-based relationships with my sponsors. Again, these relationships should be reciprocal where, in addition to the sponsor's support of me, I identify ways to help my sponsors achieve their key goals. For the relationship to thrive, I must be its driver because sponsors have a whole host of responsibilities and priorities. Their time is extremely limited.

You can do this yourself using these steps.

1. Determine who you are as a networker.

2. Decide what's important to you personally and professionally in your networking approach.

3. Figure out the key elements of a trusting relationship for you and your network contacts.

4. Identify what putting yourself out there and being proactive will look like for you.

5. Define how you'll best leverage your network members and how you'll share your background and expertise without making the conversation just about you.

6. Create personal and organizational value through the execution of your networking strategy.

Example of How You Might Start a Relationship with a Sponsor

As the director of recruiting and shared services for a national energy company, I was new to the industry and reported to the vice president of human resources who was an industry veteran. To be successful, I needed to demonstrate capability and credibility with function leaders and their teams. While making a point to consistently deliver on customer expectations and commitments as a means of demonstrating capability and credibility in a new industry, I recognized my success could be expedited with the right sponsorship.

After demonstrating my reliability through the timely, quality completion of assignments, my boss became a sponsor. This relationship helped to facilitate the successful completion of a number of high-value, politically sensitive and challenging assignments working with key company leaders and their teams. Along the way, I developed sponsor-level relationships with a number of these leaders.

After you demonstrate reliability and credibility, your approach to developing these relationships should include sharing who you are personally. This includes what you stand for and what's important to you. You can provide highlights of your career journey, and ask your sponsor to share the same. Your highlights might include your core strengths and development opportunities and needs, your career aspirations, and how you and your sponsor might work together going forward. Be sure to leave plenty of time for your sponsor to talk during this conversation. Ask them for a sense of their priorities and how you might reciprocate and support them. Clarify the frequency of the meetings and offer to schedule them.

Sample Agenda for Meeting with a Sponsor

- Discuss topics (e.g., key accomplishments, key challenges, key learnings and/or insights, career goals), provide an update, and continue to give your sponsor insights into who you are and how she/he might be most helpful.

- Ask for your sponsor's perspective. If you wish, you can do this after sharing a challenge you're facing. For example, ask your sponsor if they see an alternative approach you could take in a given situation.

- Ask your sponsor who else's perspective you should consider and who else you should add to your network. If applicable, you can ask if they'd be willing to make an introduction.

- Continue to identify how you can continue to support your sponsor's goals and priorities.

Ultimately, the objective is to become a trusted advisor to your sponsors. As a trusted advisor, you have developed the relationship and level of trust with your sponsor where, in addition to providing career advice, counsel, and influence on your behalf, she/he from time to time solicits and values your perspective and points of view. Here the relationship is of mutual benefit.

While I was an internal leadership and executive coach for a senior leader, I helped him explore a significant national role leading a client-focused segment of our business. If he was successful in that role, the position would lead to a board-level role. He was selected for the business leadership role and significantly improved business results. He asked me to help him think through how to elevate leadership effectiveness in an underperforming part of his organization. Together, we collaborated and executed a leadership development strategy to help accomplish that goal. We developed a deep, trust-based relationship that continued and was mutually beneficial. He ascended to the desired board membership, and our relationship resulted in increased visibility, credibility, and influence for me in the organization.

Trusted advisor relationships with a sponsor are not only of mutual interest but are also reciprocal. For example, the sponsor can help you by providing advice and counsel. In return, you can help the sponsor with an important need of theirs. This is a trust-based and mutually beneficial relationship.

Remember: No one can afford to be an island. Developing trusting and collaborative relationships is essential to success.

Mentors and sponsors are critical—not optional—for career success. They're the ones with whom you've developed the deepest and most trusting relationships. Again, there's no set number to have, and you simply can't have too many. Don't be shy. Ask for their expertise. Given the depth of trust in these relationships, they'll have a vested interest in your success.

If you have doubts about any relationship, remember Maya Angelou said, "When people show you who they are, believe them!" If this happens to be true for a relationship, don't trash the relationship, but at the same time, don't invest significant time and energy in relationships that are not supportive.

Personal Mantras for Engaging with Advocates

A personal mantra for use as a reminder of the importance of being proactive and intentional about identifying your sponsors and using them might be:

- "I must share my career goals and plan with mentors and sponsors and ask for what I need and/

or want in terms of advice, guidance, and counsel to be successful."

- "I must let go of my fears and be vulnerable and willing to share more of who I am and what I want with mentors and sponsors."

- "I must continue to identify, add, and sustain the right additional mentors and sponsors to my network because I can never have too many."

- "I must identify the wants and/or needs of my mentors and sponsors so that I can reciprocate by providing support to them to achieve their goals."

Checklist: Identify Sponsors

Identifying and leveraging sponsors includes sharing your career goals with them and asking for their insights and help along with proactively and intentionally identifying the key changes needed for you to shift from going it alone. Specifically, you'll want to:

- develop trusting and reciprocal relationships with mentors and sponsors;

- expand your mentor/sponsor network;

- share your career goals and plan with them and ask for their guidance and counsel;

- engage in responsible self-promotion so they are knowledgeable of your accomplishments and organizational contributions;

- believe your point of view matters and confidently share it with them;

- identify actions you're committed to do more of

or differently to embrace positive, proactive, and intentional beliefs and/or behaviors.

Take Action. Continually live
and work my plan. Commit
to proactively embrace and
execute my plan every day.

STEP 5

CHAPTER 7

Take Action

"Believe in yourself! Have faith in your abilities!
Without a humble but reasonable confidence in your
own powers you cannot be successful or happy."

—NORMAN VINCENT PEALE

"Take action" may sound easy enough at first, yet we're often
not taught how to go about taking action *successfully*. We
may also not be taught the most effective actions we can take
to make our desired career a reality. Thankfully, a study by
psychologist Gail Matthews provides evidence for the effectiveness of "accountability, commitment and writing down
one's goals." You'll notice these actions are woven into the
OWN IT process.

Matthews, a professor from Dominican University of
California, conducted a study with 149 participants from
various countries, including the US, Belgium, India, En-
gland, and Japan. The professions of participants included
vice presidents, healthcare professionals, bankers, artists,
attorneys, marketers, educators, and more. The study participants chose to pursue a variety of goals, such as increasing
income, becoming more organized, completing a project, or
learning a new skill.

A non-existent study that circulated in business circles for years—and maybe still does—inspired the real study. The non-existent study suggested only 3% of graduates from a Harvard Business School class (sometimes Yale was mentioned instead) wrote specific goals for the future. After a twenty-year period, the story went, those who wrote down their goals earned ten times more than those graduates who didn't. Impressive results! Too bad they weren't true.

Matthews noted that "extensive reviews of the research literature by me and by Steven Kraus (a social psychologist from Harvard) as well as investigative reporting by *Fast Company* magazine revealed that no such study had ever been done." She wrote that the "widespread mention of this non-existent study in business circles as well as the need for research" provided the drive to conduct *actual* research and a study. Her research focused on how "goal achievement is influenced by writing goals, committing to goal-directed actions, and being accountable for those actions" (Matthews 2007).

Participants in the real study were assigned to one of five groups. The summary of each group is listed below.

- Group 1—unwritten goal;
- Group 2—written goal;
- Group 3—written goal and action commitments;
- Group 4—written goal, action commitments to a friend;
- Group 5—written goal, action commitments and progress reports to a friend.

In the end, Group 5 achieved more than all of the other groups. Additionally, the team's analysis revealed that "the mean achievement score for Groups 2-5 combined was significantly higher than Group 1." In other words, those with the written goal performed better (Matthews 2007).

What Helps You Most in Taking Action to Achieve Your Goals?

The study detailed main takeaways and provides evidence for writing down your goals, committing to action, and being held accountable. The conclusions of the study indicated the following.

- **Writing down your goals**: Those who wrote their goals accomplished significantly more than those who did not (Matthews 2007).

- **OWN IT process tool**: The templates available in the resources section guide you through developing and writing down your goals and related actions and being accountable by sharing them and your progress and achievements with trusted advisors.

- **Public commitment**: Participants who sent their commitments to a friend accomplished significantly more than those who wrote action commitments or did not write their goals (Matthews 2007).

- **OWN IT process tool**: Speak with your advocates about your commitments after you go through the OWN IT process to confirm your Living Career Action Plan.

- **Accountability**: Matthews noted that "those who sent weekly progress reports to their friend accomplished *significantly more* than those who had unwritten goals, wrote their goals, formulated action commitments or sent those action commitments to a friend."

- **OWN IT process tool**: Arrange with a colleague or trusted advocate to regularly share and discuss your challenges, progress, and achievements, as well as things to do more of or differently for greater success.

The Benefits of a Career Plan and Self-Reflection

Your career plan is a living, formal statement of what's important to you in your career, including your career goals, actions, resources, challenges, metrics, and timeline. A plan helps you define your career direction and describes your priorities and approach to achieving your goals. A formal plan creates a sense of direction, urgency, and accountability to act. In the absence of a plan, your career direction and goals are just informal thoughts. As we can observe from the study results above, formalizing our thoughts in writing makes them more real and worthy of pursuit.

A Living Career Action Plan confirms your most current, desired career destination and roadmap for getting there and requires:

- continuous self-reflection: what's possible, what's working, what change is needed;
- updates to reflect your most current career goals and actions;
- confirmation of the experience and learning goals to be achieved and of the key support resources you'll leverage to achieve your goals;
- identification of the key challenges you'll face and

how you'll navigate them along with the metrics you'll use to confirm your successful journey;

- your timeline and milestones for achieving your career goals and actions.

"Taking action" is the execution, actualization, and sustainability step of the OWN IT process. By execution and actualization, I mean being proactive, committed, and intentional about taking the specific actions needed to achieve specific career plan goals. "Sustainability" includes the maintenance actions needed, including:

- periodic self-reflection on what's working or may need to change;
- continuous learning and growth, both formally and on the job;
- retaining, nurturing, and seeking counsel from key coach, colleague, mentor, and sponsor relationships;
- updating your Living Career Action Plan to reflect your most current career destination and path.

Self-reflection creates space for you to put yourself first and think about who you are and what you want from your career. It's an activity that is ongoing and is an opportunity to do periodic check-ins with yourself to confirm your plan is meeting your interests and passions, as well as that your career is on course. If changes are needed, you'll know and make any needed course corrections. This possibility is to be expected because your desired destination may evolve as you do. So, calendarizing ongoing self-reflection time is a must to assess whether you're on your desired career course.

Like most things in life, including your career, you can

control some aspects and not others. Having and executing a Living Career Action Plan is energizing, builds self-confidence, and results in strong impact and performance.

A Successful Plan Helps You Do the Following

- Create and confirm a desired career direction.
- Identify and confirm a desired destination.
- Generate a proactive, intentional, and planful career focus.
- Serve as a career compass against which to consider prospective career opportunities.
- Encourage being a curious, continuous, and humble learner.
- Require continuous self-awareness and self-reflection to ensure you're on your desired path.
- Ensure growing and sustaining reciprocal relationships with advocates including, coaches, colleagues, mentors, and sponsors.
- Reinforce an inclusive leadership style.
- Increase influence and impact while adding value.
- Confirm alignment with your Personal Purpose.
- Encourage planful growth and the leveraging of your strengths.
- Focus on the planful addressing of your development gaps.
- Create a strong sense of self and self-belief.
- Focus on destination and learning.
- Encourage you to reciprocate by bringing along

coaches and colleagues and mentoring and/or sponsoring others.

- Commit to being mindful of your legacy (what you want to be known for and how you'd like to be remembered).

Living a planless, meandering, and situational career offers only a passive approach to your career; gives you only a "job availability" focus rather than a "career destination" focus; subjects you to someone else's needs and makes you part of someone else's game plan; limits your influence to what others need from you; limits you to a near-term increased visibility and lifestyle focus rather than a career-destination focus; limits you to situational learning based on the opportunities offered to you; and encourages only transactional advocate relationships.

Without an identified destination and plan, you'll risk living a career of whimsy and directional uncertainty based on the wants and needs of others rather than your own.

Focus on a career *destination* instead of job availability.

Success requires a mind shift from mistaken beliefs to continuous self-reflection, learning, adaptation, commitment, and execution because nothing desirable happens without the consistent application of these key actions.

- Embracing positive, proactive, and intentional

beliefs helps you believe that you will be successful by listening to your positive internal voice. *If I don't believe in myself, who else will?*

- Sharing and discussing my career interests, preferences, and Living Action Plan goals continually with coaches, colleagues, mentors, and sponsors regardless of who they are or what they look like. *They can't help me if they don't know what I want.*

Additionally, they incentivize you to seek the advice, counsel, and insights from trusted advocates on the items below.

- My progress and challenges achieving my living plan goals and their alignment with my desired career destination.

- Prospective course corrections to my goals and plan, which reflect changes in my learnings, interests, and preferences.

- Feedback on how others, including leaders and peers, are experiencing me.

- Personal development opportunities.

These actions will help you confirm your destination and commit to being your best self every day and adding the most possible value to the organization. They will also help you build a following by giving back and sharing what you've learned when you serve as a mentor and sponsor for others.

A Living Career Action Plan is an antidote to thinking you can't influence your outcome.

Those who subscribe to passive and erroneous beliefs or behaviors likely believe they don't have the leverage in the organization to influence the desired outcome. The antidote is developing and executing a Living Career Action Plan. Such a plan can reduce your inertia or fears, increase self-confidence, and set an expectation for success. Just as the research above showed, writing down your commitments helps you achieve them.

The idea of looking down the road into the future can be overwhelming. And yet the process can become more difficult without thinking through each step. Without investing the time to envision your career destination and develop a plan to reach it, you'll remain on a path that won't feel satisfying.

Developing and executing a thoughtful, comprehensive plan is not a race. No shortcuts to executing a successful plan exist. Plan creation and execution takes self-reflection, honesty, intellectual humility, commitment, focus, proactive action, and intentionality.

What's Important to Do and Know When Taking Action?

Self-Reflection

Self-reflection is critical to ensure you are traveling your desired career direction and path. It requires the discipline to regularly calendarize time to review your plan and its execution for fit and alignment with your purpose, desired direction, learnings and development, and opportunities to add value. Self-reflection provides the opportunity to maximize your valuable time and energy by either continuing your current course or making the necessary changes in your plan or its execution to more effectively pursue your desired career path and destination.

Honesty

Honesty is important to ensure that you're telling yourself the truth and making career decisions that are truly in your best interests rather than someone else's. So, it's important to select a direction or role that is aligned with your career destination and strengthens your portfolio of knowledge and skills, rather than taking on a role simply because it's available or because, politically, someone else thinks it's a good move.

If a role change is politically advisable, be sure to negotiate up front the expectations and benefits of the change including the length of the assignment, criteria for success, the leadership support you can expect during the assignment, and what your subsequent assignment will be to get you back on your desired career journey.

Intellectual Humility

Intellectual humility is an important asset for meaningful learning and growth during the course of your career journey. It encourages looking at each new role as an opportunity to learn new things rather than to lean more on the knowledge you already possess. This doesn't mean that you let go of what you know. Rather, this means you leverage current knowledge and focus more on new learning and being comfortable delegating what's known in order to learn new things, add value in your current role, and strengthen your preparation and candidacy for the next role.

Commitment

This chapter started with scientific research that backs the necessity of public commitments. Commitment is the engine that drives career plan execution and actualization. Without commitment, a plan is just words on a page. Commitment is the "yes, I will" that unleashes action in the forms of focus, proactive action, and intentionality. Without a career plan, commitment is an engine at rest. Similarly, without commitment, then focus, proactive action, and intentionality are inactive and in the "off" position.

Focus

Focus empowers you to be single-minded in your desire to pay exclusive attention to particular tasks without being distracted by competing interests. This allows you to identify and bring to bear the right resources to successfully complete the desired task.

Proactive Action

Proactive action means you personally take the necessary action(s) to make your desired career outcomes happen rather than wait for them to happen on their own. In this way, you make sure that you're doing everything you reasonably can to successfully achieve the outcomes you want rather than leaving things to chance. In this way, even if things don't quite turn out the way you want, you can say that you did all you could to achieve success and still can make needed course corrections.

Intentionality

Intentionality means acting with deliberation and purpose to achieve a desired outcome. Accordingly, you're clear on which action(s) you're prepared to take versus not take. Therefore, your actions are intentional rather than random. Intentionality increases the likelihood of achieving the desired career outcomes you want.

❧

Your Living Career Action Plan should reflect quality and thoroughness over speed. A quality career plan, path, and destination should genuinely reflect your evolving learnings, passions, interests, and preferences.

To serve you well, your career plan should be thorough and comprehensive. This means your Living Career Action Plan should reflect your most current goals, actions, desired resources, challenges, metrics, timeline, and milestones. Additionally, you should also capture advocates who can be most helpful. You shouldn't assume that your career journey will be linear. As I mentioned previously, you may decide to move laterally to gain desired knowledge and skills to position yourself as a stronger candidate for a desired role. Consequently, you should plan and be open to considering lateral and/or vertical career moves that are aligned with your career destination and strengthen your knowledge and skills. Finally, the thoroughness and comprehensiveness of your plan will require you to be reasonable and honest with yourself in terms of your desired career destination and path and the speed by which to get there. Additionally, investing in yourself and your career—by defining your career possibilities and options, and by updating and executing your living career plan—is a key part of the Own It process and essential to a successful, fulfilling career journey.

Checklist: The Positive and Proactive Mindset to Have

- Maintaining a positive, optimistic, and confident mindset about you and your career and replacing negative internal voice messages with positive ones;

- sharing your Living Career Action Plan and interests with coaches, colleagues, mentors, and sponsors who are in a position to be supportive and influential on your behalf;

- keeping mentors and sponsors up to date on your accomplishments and asking for their guidance on efforts to successfully navigate your challenges;

- seeking and owning your feedback and leveraging it to deepen key relationships and increase your value and impact;

- focusing on being your best self every day and giving back by mentoring and sponsoring others.

Remember: A plan will be merely words on a page without your commitment and execution. So, focus on what you can control and try not to worry about what you can't. An indicator of exceptional leadership beyond exceptional performance happens by developing a following among team members and others who have grown and developed from your leadership and who've benefited from your mentorship or sponsorship.

Personal Mantras for Taking Action

A personal mantra for use as a reminder of what's important for you to be proactive and intentional about taking action might be:

- "I will only be successful if I partner and reciprocate with my coaches, colleagues, mentors, and sponsors."
- "I will be successful if I proactively commit to making intellectual humility and executing my Living Career Action Plan a daily habit."
- "I genuinely believe I am capable and deserve to have the career I want."
- "I am confident in my ability to successfully navigate prospective career challenges and achieve my career goals."

Checklist: The Mistaken Beliefs and Behaviors to Let Go

The ideas to let go include believing the following:

- Having a career plan will ensure I achieve my career goals;
- Believing I won't be successful because my story is already written or preordained;
- No matter what I do, someone else owns and controls my success;
- Seeking guidance and counsel from others who look like me may not be helpful;
- Keeping a low profile will somehow put me in a better position to succeed.

What Else Should I Be Mindful of When Taking Action?

As you may recall, I shared a personal story earlier about when I reached a decision point in my career. I had to decide whether to pursue another human resources leadership opportunity or formalize a new career direction. I attended a "Life Forward" session at the Hudson Institute and prepared a Life Plan that led me to become a leadership and executive coach, which I determined to be my new career destination. With the Hudson Life Plan, I considered my life roles, including as a family member, friend, and community member. I also considered my career progress to date along with areas for personal and professional growth and mastery. The theme for this plan was, "My Journey of Sustained Self-Actualization and Happiness." This Life Plan, followed by the preparation of my Personal Balance Sheet, was a key ingredient in preparing, executing, and living my Living Career Action Plan as a coach. To this day, I revisit my Hudson Life Plan periodically to reflect on and track my journey and ensure I'm living the career I want as a coach and to ensure I'm feeling fulfilled and continuing to contribute and give back to clients and others in the ways I want.

What's Required for Success

Taking action by continually living and working your plan and committing to proactively embracing and executing your plan every day will require you to:

- maintain a healthy self-confidence;
- replace negative self-messages with positive ones;
- share career plan progress regularly with your

coaches, colleagues, mentors, and sponsors and
solicit their advice and counsel;

- keep your living career plan current so it reflects
your current interests, passions, and growth;

- engage regularly in self-reflection to ensure you
execute your plan every day;

- identify one to three actions you're committed
to do more of or differently to embrace positive,
proactive, and intentional beliefs or behaviors to
identify sponsors and create mutually productive
relationships.

CHAPTER 8

Story Traps, Mindset, and the Importance of Continuous Learning

"Learning is the beginning of wealth. Learning
is the beginning of health. Learning is the
beginning of spirituality. Searching and learning
is where the miracle process all begins."

—JIM ROHN

A mindset is a habitual, characteristic mental attitude that determines how you will interpret and respond to situations. A key to continued learning and growth is to consider your mindset as a learner. Earlier, I mentioned how Carol Dweck and her research revealed that two implicit theories of intelligence exist—a growth mindset and a fixed mindset. With a growth mindset, people view their skills and intelligence as improvable. Those with fixed mindsets believe that you're born with a fixed quantity of intelligence and that your personality is set in stone.

When you believe your skills and intelligence *can* be expanded, you have a growth mindset. You're likely to be more motivated to engage in continuous learning while supporting curiosity, intentionality, and intellectual humility. With a growth mindset, you have a green light to pursue your learning interests because your learning potential is yours to determine and own. You determine your learning direction and focus, which are likely to include knowledge and skills aligned with your career goals and destination.

On the other hand, a fixed mindset limits your learning potential, suggesting that your intelligence and personality are preordained at birth. With a fixed mindset, if you're smart, kind of smart, or not smart, you believe you were born that way and will remain that way forever. When we use labels like "smart," "not smart," "high potential," or "low potential," we reinforce this thinking. Alternatively, a growth mindset combined with effort, self-reflection, and intentionality will likely lead to learning and performance success in your current and future roles throughout your career journey.

Mindtraps, which are ineffective ways of thinking and responding to situations, also impact learning and performance. They can impede and negatively affect the quality of your thinking and decision-making. This reflexive way of thinking and acting is incompatible with continuous learning and a growth mindset that requires curiosity, intentionality, and intellectual humility.

Five Main Mindtraps to Avoid

Jennifer Garvey Berger is a leadership expert and author and works with senior leaders around the world. In her book, *Unlocking Leadership Mindtraps: How to Thrive in Complexity*, she identifies five potential mindtraps that those in, or pursuing, leadership roles need to avoid to successfully navigate complexity:

1. Being trapped by simple stories: Your desire for a simple story blinds you to a real one.

2. Being trapped by rightness: Just because you *feel* it's right, doesn't mean it *is* right.

3. Being trapped by agreement: Longing for alignment robs you of good ideas.

4. Being trapped by control: Trying to take charge strips you of influence.

5. Being trapped by ego: Shackled to who you are now, you can't reach for who you'll be next.

Common desires related to these mindtraps are for speedy and transactional resolutions as well as for resolutions to be peaceful, predictable, and personally satisfying. Unfortunately, the desire for speedy, feel-good resolutions versus thoughtful resolutions often don't result in the best outcomes. During my career, I've fallen prey to several of these mindtraps, including simple stories, trapped by rightness, trapped by agreement, and trapped by control.

My Story of Being Trapped in Simple Stories

I've been guilty of saying yes and agreeing to take on assignments with unreasonable time frames for completion. That time pressure put me in the frame of mind of trying to keep things simple. To avoid feeling overwhelmed, I limited the information I took into account in an effort to keep the project or task manageable. This meant that any solution I might develop would be based on limited information with a limited likelihood of success. At that time in my career, I didn't have the courage to push back and negotiate a more reasonable time frame for the assignment. I painted myself into a corner.

As a result, my proposed solution was not my best work and resulted in rework. I missed the agreed-upon completion date. Fortunately, I learned from the experience and going forward only said yes after negotiating reasonable time frames. That gave me time to research the full story and not put myself into the situation of feeling the need to settle for a simple story when feeling overwhelmed.

The Trap of Rightness

The need to be right in the eyes of others is a seductive trap. At times, in an effort to save face, I have been unwilling to admit my misjudgments when, clearly, I miscalculated part of a project. Clearly, my pride got in the way. This resulted in convoluted explanations on my part to avoid the embarrassment of admitting my error to save face in an effort to be perceived as confident in my rightness by colleagues. Rather than be perceived as inflexible and untrustworthy, I've learned it's better to share your points of view while remaining willing to accept the more informed insights and opinions of others. Then, you're perceived as a collaborative contributor and learner. No matter what, don't let your pride lock you into being right.

The Agreement Trap

When up against tight timelines on assignments, I've been tempted, against my better judgment, "to agree to almost anything" with colleagues to keep the peace and reach agreement rather than engage in healthy debate in order to move forward on an assignment. There was undue focus by me on agreement rather than the assignment objective, the required work, and desired outcome of the assignment. This was a bad approach that led to wasted time, resources, and significant rework before finally taking the right path for project success. Unfortunately, the assignment results were delivered embarrassingly late and, for a time, negatively impacted the reputations of project participants. This trap can also result in frayed relationships.

The Control Trap

For me, control is about there being no surprises and that I've hopefully considered the alternatives to my desired outcome. It's taken me a while to realize it, but I can't control all the things I'd like. I can control some aspects and not others. I've learned to identify as best I can what I can and can't control. For what I can't control, I try to identify how I or someone I have a relationship with may provide me with insight on how we might be able to influence the situation. Then, I'll make an action plan for moving forward, controlling what I can, anticipating challenges and, if possible, influencing what I can't control to achieve my desired outcome.

∽

Falling prey to the sustained employment of these mindtraps will negatively affect the quality of your learning, decision-making, and likely limit your long-term career success. Avoiding these mindtraps while employing a growth mindset will equip you to learn from successes and failures and prepare you to effectively apply your newfound knowledge going forward. This will encourage you to embrace learning as an opportunity to continually refine, polish, and expand your knowledge and capabilities with humility and curiosity and an interest and willingness to share them collaboratively for the greater good.

A continuous learning orientation, together with a growth mindset, will equip you to detect and fend off falling prey to the negative effects of prospective mindtraps. Maintaining an openness to continuous learning and the avoidance of mindtraps will support the development and execution of your Living Career Action Plan and lead to meaningful contributions and success along your career journey.

CHAPTER 9

The Entire OWN IT Process—How Sheila Owned Her Career

> "True happiness involves the full use of one's power and talents."
>
> **—JOHN W. GARDNER**

> "Things do not happen. Things are made to happen."
>
> **—JOHN F. KENNEDY**

This chapter puts the entire OWN IT process together by sharing the story of a POC woman who, after wishing and hoping for the desired career progress, decided to take more ownership of her career. I've named her Sheila, and her story is a combination of member stories from a cohort of female clients I've coached. Sheila was a talented and capable client of mine, and the details of her experience have been changed to a certain extent to protect her privacy. She was a business process consultant at a global business operations consulting firm. She trusted the firm's leadership to inform and direct her career and hoped that would culminate in a promotion to partner at some point.

Sheila's Initial Career Direction

Sheila joined the firm right out of college after a summer spent interning in their systems and operations (S&O) practice. Her initial take was that S&O played to her analytical orientation and desire to help clients improve their internal operations. The firm offered a predetermined career opportunity and path from entry-level staff member to the manager level. Sheila started as an entry-level staff member on project teams. Over eight years, she steadily advanced to a senior staff member level. Later, she reached manager and then senior manager. Her next promotion would be to partner, which was her original aspiration. Her career was progressing as hoped.

The "Up or Out" Firm Culture

The firm's demographics included primarily white males in a highly competitive "up or out" culture. The "up or out" culture meant that you either continually moved up and proved your worth via promotions or you'd be asked to leave the firm. The firm continually recruited new staff who were diverse, smart, and goal-oriented with proven track records of academic and personal success. Sheila fit that profile and distinguished herself as a valued contributor. Employees who exceeded goals and expectations were ranked higher in terms of recognition, rewards, and promotions. Sheila was in that category. The challenge for Sheila was developing a network of trusted advocates who would provide timely and necessary advice and counsel. Initially, her network was the result of having led successful client projects. Ultimately, she realized that having a valuable and supportive network of trusted advocates would require her to be more intentional and proactive to successfully identify, develop, and sustain trusting relationships with her coaches, colleagues, mentors, and sponsors.

The Successes

Sheila possessed excellent client relationship management (CRM) skills. She was an active listener and connected with each client on a personal level. This helped her quickly build trust with mid- to senior-level client representatives. Sheila had a genuine interest in understanding the client's operations, culture, capabilities, competitors, and challenges. This energized her and played into her desire to help client organizations significantly improve their operations.

She made it a point to understand the client's business, operations, market, and competitors, including their competitors' strengths and weaknesses versus those of her client. She was also effective at creating an inclusive and collaborative culture for her project team. As leader, Sheila set the expectation for team members to be independent and critical thinkers (i.e., to analyze information to make reasoned judgements and decisions) to ensure that the best ideas were surfaced and considered. To that end, her leadership style is best described as an "asking" rather than a "telling" style. So, she led her team by *asking* team members questions for which she didn't necessarily have the answers.

This resulted in her creating and sustaining a desirable team culture by soliciting the input and perspectives of team members on project planning, execution, and progress. This inclusive and respectful approach with team members was fueled by her desire to ensure that the best ideas, approaches, and course corrections to client project work weren't solely hers to identify and, instead, were continually surfaced and considered by the team before making decisions.

Edgar H. Schein, in his book *Humble Inquiry: The Gentle Art of Asking Instead of Telling*, talks about the importance of communication by leaders. In particular, he emphasizes that leaders use a specific communications strategy with those who report directly to them. He mentions that there's a tendency for leaders to tell team members what the leader thinks they need to know. However, he points out that this behavior can shut team members down and prevent the generation of bold new ideas, as well as preclude the development of team member flexibility and agility. Instead, Schein's humble inquiry approach helps a leader build relationships based on mutual curiosity and interest.

Sheila's leadership skills and capabilities enabled her and her team to consistently meet and often exceed client expectations. Clients considered her a trusted advisor.

Step 1 of the OWN IT Process in Action

Own My Career

Sheila followed step one to take more ownership of her career. With the opportunity to become a partner a real possibility, she reflected on her career path. Thus far, the firm had predetermined her path from that entry-level staff member position eight years earlier to senior manager. She began to think about what she wanted to do if she made partner. She wondered:

- What kind of partner would she want to be?
- What consulting specialty would she prefer?
- Would she stay in S&O? If not, where would she want to be?

Eight years at the firm had flown by. This self-reflection helped her realize that she needed to spend time answering these, and other, questions to help her identify a career destination and path of *her* own choosing. She'd need to develop and execute a Living Career Action Plan to confirm her career direction and achieve her goals. She realized that she would need the right trusted advocates to provide her with timely, targeted guidance, advice, and counsel.

Sheila was startled to reexamine her thinking and observe that she had expected the firm's predetermined career path to provide her career satisfaction and fulfillment. In effect, she'd delegated responsibility for her career to the firm. Thankfully, this self-reflection led her to embrace the positive, proactive, and intentional beliefs and behaviors of "identifying her career direction, goals, and actions with intention and passion" and "confirming her needs and passions when preparing her Living Career Action Plan."

Step 2 of the OWN IT Process in Action

Be Who I am More—Not Less

Even during her summer internship, Sheila knew that she'd be one of the few women and POC at the firm if she kept working there after graduation. To distinguish herself and be successful, she knew she'd have to be an exceptional performer and also develop supportive relationships with peers, colleagues, and leaders. As part of her efforts to develop relationships, she reached out to her peers, colleagues, and other POC in the firm to share her experiences, learn from theirs, and hear more about the unwritten rules within the firm's culture. She sensed that her long-term success would require the development of relationships beyond her immediate team members and managers to include leaders who could coach, mentor, or sponsor her in her career aspirations.

In the early years, she focused on learning, performing, and relationship development. Her success relied on knowing and effectively leveraging the firm's protocols and systems related to her project work. The firm offered her training and development, and she took full advantage of these opportunities to expand her knowledge and capabilities. She continued to focus on performing well and reaching out and introducing herself to people. She had a serious, results-oriented side to her along with a social and engaging side. To fit in, she knew that she would need to leverage her serious and results-oriented side with others. As she continued to develop relationships with team members and others, she was able to bring the more social and engaging side of her personality into the workplace to deepen her working relationships.

As she continued to experience success with client presentations and leading projects, she gained the respect and confidence of her colleagues. Her performance and personal growth were notable, and she was promoted to senior staff after two years. The senior staff role included more client-facing engagements. Her promotion into this role reflected the confidence and trust the firm's clients and team managers had in Sheila's capabilities.

Despite her continued performance success, she felt she was under a microscope more than her counterparts. This drove her to be a bit of a perfectionist, which was exhausting both physically and mentally. She didn't want to be known as the woman and POC who didn't measure up and failed. In challenging times, she sought encouragement and support from her network of trusted advocates, including POC who were senior managers and partners in the firm. They talked her off the ledge from being a perfectionist and emphasized focusing on "good enough" rather than perfection. They counseled her on the importance of self-care to avoid burnout.

Sheila was clear that, as a POC, she continually had to prove herself and that nothing would be given to her. Her ultimate career success would require her to effectively leverage her knowledge, capabilities, experiences, and relationships. This would require her to be a continuous learner. She would also need to be proactive, focused, and intentional to reach her career destination and path.

At the same time, she wanted to be herself at work. To do that, she would have to feel more comfortable being herself. She followed the second step of the OWN IT process to be more of herself at work while embracing more positive beliefs and useful behaviors. As her feeling of comfort grew, she began to think of her long-term career direction and desires.

Step 3 of the OWN IT Process in Action

Decide Now Is the Time

Sheila's initial career destination was to become a partner and, at some point, a practice leader. Upon further reflection, her desires became more specific. She hoped to become a senior partner running a significant segment of the firm's business.

She wanted increased exposure to the firm's global practices and operations. For this, she considered a career destination that included becoming a global business or practice leader for the firm.

To achieve her desired career destination, she would need continued success securing and leading client projects, which would require expanding her knowledge of global, industrial, and regional economic trends impacting client businesses and operations. The more deeply she thought about her desired career direction, path, and destination after making partner, the more she understood the importance of taking direct responsibility for her career. She understood that relying less on the firm to decide her direction would only benefit her.

Sheila received her promotion to partner and observed how important annually updating her Personal Balance Sheet had been in preparing and executing a current Living Career Action Plan to reach her goal of becoming a partner.

Sheila's Initial Personal Balance Sheet Process

A copy of Sheila's completed current Personal Balance Sheet is presented in the resources section of this book.

To formalize her career direction and path, Sheila first committed to reflect on and prepare a Personal Balance Sheet capturing key areas for reflection and reference for creating a meaningful initial Living Career Action Plan.

Key elements of her Personal Balance Sheet included:

- A statement of Sheila's Personal Purpose that reflected what she considered the key drivers in her life. Her career vision statement helped her look strategically at her career and life's desired direction.

- Her values statement reflected her values and their degree of positive or negative alignment with her purpose, Life's Vision, and current career experiences and direction.

- Her career experiences statement inventoried her most valued career experiences to date and served as a reminder of those experiences.

- Her significant career accomplishments statement captured her significant accomplishments thus far.

- Her professional strengths statement captured the major strengths that helped her achieve the successes she's had.

- A list of her important development opportunities helped her understand the critical development needs that would strengthen her potential for continued success on her career journey.

- Her treasured relationships included trusted advocates (coaches, colleagues, mentors, and sponsors) and her Personal Board of Directors.

- Her career preferences ranked her most important preferences when considering career opportunities and roles.

- Her major career goals included those focused on achieving her desired career.

- Her commitment to self-management stated her commitment to doing the personal work necessary to achieve the career she desired.

As she worked through the OWN IT process, Sheila decided that, as per step three, "now was the time to focus her efforts and relentlessly pursue her career goals." She let go of her passive beliefs and behaviors about career planning and pursuit, including the notion that working hard and being smart was enough by itself for a successful career. She let go of the idea that the organization and its leaders knew what was best and that asking for help displayed weakness.

Instead, Sheila embraced positive, proactive, and intentional beliefs and behaviors, including the belief that she would live a life of purpose, confirm her career direction, develop and share her Living Career Action Plan with her trusted advocates, use her plan, and ask for advice and counsel from her mentors and sponsors.

Sheila considered the information and insights from these two tools against the career direction and impact she wanted to make as a partner going forward. This realization underscored the importance of viewing her balance sheet and career plan as living documents to be revisited to confirm and inform possible changes in her future direction and destination. This confirmed for her the importance of having and executing a living plan instead of becoming a part of someone else's plan.

Developing and identifying the key takeaways from her Personal Balance Sheet assessment helped Sheila see that her knowledge, experience, capabilities, passions, and interests showed that she excelled at developing strong trusted advisor-level client relationships. She confirmed her passion for being an inclusive leader of team members focused on the successful implementation of client solutions. This reinforced her change management orientation and focus, ensuring client solutions were aligned with other interrelated client organizational functions, processes, and systems.

Sheila determined that her desired career destination as a partner would be to make the case to become the S&O practice leader for change management. Identifying this as her desired career destination helped her begin to think deeply and qualitatively about the content of her Living Career Action Plan, including key goals, actions, resources and advocates, challenges, metrics, and timeline. A copy of Sheila's Initial Living Career Action Plan is presented in the resources section of this book.

Step 4 of the OWN IT Process in Action

Identify My Trusted Advocates
and Seek Their Counsel

Sheila followed step four to identify and develop trust-based relationships with advocates (including coaches, colleagues, mentors, and sponsors) and ask them for insights.

Over eight years, Sheila had developed a reliable and supportive network of trusted advocates. These relationships were primarily developed in connection with client projects she'd successfully worked on or led. As she thought about the prospect of her career destination beyond just making partner, she began to put her passions and interests first. She recognized that having the career she wanted meant honoring her passions and interests and making the case with sponsors and leveraging deep and trusting relationships with them. The process of developing her initial Living Career Action Plan triggered her to consider those currently in her network whom she considered to be her most trusted mentors and/or sponsors. She sought to expand her network

CRAFT AND OWN YOUR CAREER

and initiated conversations with her network members to help identify leaders who might be potential sponsors. Next, she committed to developing her Living Career Action Plan and sharing it with her existing network members for feedback. Meanwhile, she prepared to share it with new network members, in particular, her sponsors.

Finally, Sheila identified a Personal Board of Directors (PBOD) of three to five of her most trusted advocates for both real-time tactical and strategic guidance and counsel. They would help her with important issues, including her personal brand, performance feedback, career direction, and options. This led to the development of a strategy and related actions to continue to thoughtfully expand her network of advocates, coaches, mentors, and sponsors.

Sheila's approach to identifying the right trusted advocates was a multistep process starting with first identifying prospective network members who were successful leaders. She screened those people with whom she had value and trust-based relationships along with those who:

- offered broad firm and practice knowledge;
- could advise her on power and politics within the firm;
- knew her well and would provide candid feedback and tell her the truth;
- could help her expand her network with the right people;
- were willing to become mentors or sponsors if they weren't already;
- would be excellent members of her PBOD.

Through conversations with her PBOD members, Sheila

identified ways to strengthen existing sponsor relationships by identifying opportunities to make them more reciprocal rather than transactional. She did this by finding ways to help these sponsors accomplish their own goals. In one example of this reciprocity, one of Sheila's sponsors used their personal political capital to have a conversation with a senior firm leader to make the case for a role change for Sheila that would expand her knowledge, growth, and value to the firm and its systems and operations and change management clients. The conversation was successful. In return, her sponsor asked Sheila, whose team leadership and coaching skills were well known, to meet with and share her experiences with the sponsor's direct reports and share her "leader as coach" approach with leadership, as per Edgar Schien's humble inquiry idea of leading team members by asking rather than telling.

She shared her thoughts about her career direction, Living Career Action Plan, path, and destination at least annually for discussion and feedback with her PBOD. They critiqued and helped her fine-tune her plan and also discussed plan progress and performance, knowledge and skills development requirements to achieve her career goals. With this invaluable input from her PBOD, Sheila executed her updated Living Career Action Plan.

Five Challenges Sheila Experienced in Navigating Her Career Destination

As a woman and POC, a challenge Sheila faced was winning and sustaining the support of senior leadership and successfully demonstrating her ability and willingness to challenge the status quo, engage in healthy debates, and drive meaningful change for her clients and profitable engagements for her business practice and the firm. A second challenge for her was continuing to contribute significantly to the firm's success, including winning and sustaining the respect and collaborative support of senior leaders and counterparts. She also had to manage earning and sustaining the trust and respect of clients while earning and sustaining the respect, trust, and commitment of her teams in order to deliver value to clients. Finally, she was challenged to continuously expand her industry/business knowledge, thought leader relationships, and her capabilities.

A copy of Sheila's current Personal Balance Sheet and Living Career Action Plan is available in the resources section of this book.

Step 5 of the OWN IT Process in Action

Take Action

Sheila executed and measured her career progress in step five, which is to "take action, continually live and work the plan and commit to proactively embrace and execute my plan every day." Sheila actively tracked her goal progress. This included goals achieved, the timely achievement of desired learning, development, and experiential outcomes. She reviewed the degree to which she effectively leveraged available resources and her network of trusted advocates and received her desired level of support. She assessed how successfully she had navigated the challenges reflected in her Living Career Action Plan, including how well she overcame the challenges and what she learned from each experience. Sheila regularly assessed her success with meeting and staying on schedule against the near-term, medium-term, and long-term milestone timelines she set for herself.

How Sheila Ensured She Was on the Right Track

Since we worked together on her career plan, Sheila regularly takes time to reflect on the degree of satisfaction, growth, and fulfillment she is currently experiencing on her career journey to ensure she's on her desired path. Additionally, she reviews her most current Personal Balance Sheet and Living Career Action Plan at least annually for fit and alignment with her current learnings, passions, and interests. Based on those steps, she updates her Living Career Action Plan.

Next, Sheila confirms her current understanding of her role and responsibilities as a leader along with the corresponding expectations. Then, she confirms her understanding of her career path and compares that to her desired career destination expressed in her most current Living Career Action Plan. Finally, she shares her desired career destination with her bosses, advocates, and PBOD to confirm whether her preferred destination is feasible within, and hopefully beyond, the S&O business practice.

If not, she'll discuss with bosses and advocates, including her PBOD, the prospect of pursuing her career path and destination elsewhere in the firm. If confirmed, she'll update her Living Career Action Plan to capture her modified career goals, actions, resources, challenges, metrics, and timeline. If not confirmed, she'll likely consider using her Personal Balance Sheet and Living Career Action Plan as tools to explore options outside the firm.

In fact, this annual review of her Living Career Action Plan with advocates and her PBOD led to Sheila's decision to move from a change management practice leader to become a broader business leader in the firm. This insight was the result of revising her Living Career Action Plan to reflect her desire to change her career direction, path, and destination along with the input from bosses, advocates, and her PBOD.

What Sheila Learned and Would Do Differently Next Time

Sheila would focus and commit to "own" her career sooner and be more proactive and intentional about growing and leveraging her network sooner. Having a Living Career Action Plan in place provided Sheila a sense of independence and confidence and confirmed her career vision and direction for the future, as well as a destination and path to get there.

As a woman and POC, her Living Career Action Plan provided firm footing for her to be who she was as a leader. She recognized that colleagues may have made assumptions and held beliefs about her (e.g., assuming and/or believing Sheila was an Equal Employment Opportunity or diversity hire) and may have viewed her promotion to partner as unearned no matter what.

Earlier in her career with the firm, she would have allowed these perceived assumptions and beliefs to affect her self-confidence, self-belief, judgements, and actions. Now, with a clear, desired career destination, strong self-confidence, demonstrated successful leadership and client capabilities, and an effective network of trusted advocates, the assumptions and beliefs of others are no longer an immobilizing/demoralizing concern.

Sheila's Outcome from the OWN IT Process

For Sheila, the promotion to an S&O change management partner and then to a broader business leader confirmed her contributions and value to her clients, the firm, and herself. An important source of her self-belief and confidence was fueled and confirmed by her Living Career Action Plan. By having a current career plan developed and in place, she felt a sense of calm and confidence about her future.

After she engaged in and experienced the value of the OWN IT process, she also made it a point to reach out to coach and mentor individual members of her teams. The OWN IT process was working and continued to work for Sheila over her career.

How to Identify and Assess New Opportunities in Your Organization

Although organizations may or may not have a wealth of career opportunities, the reality is they are typically driven by the needs of the business rather than by individual employee career desires. You'll want to proactively and intentionally define your desired career direction and path at your organization, which can serve as a career direction compass. With a clearly defined career direction and path, you can assess the fit and alignment of existing, new, and upcoming position opportunities with your desired direction.

Share Your Desired Career Direction

All position opportunities may not be formally posted or communicated. Consequently, when that's the case, the organization may select someone else for the role you would have wanted. So, be sure to share your desired career direction with trusted advisors and decision-makers so that they're aware of your career interests and desired path.

Ask Specific Questions

When assessing fit, the question is: "Does this opportunity enhance my knowledge, skills, and experiences while moving me closer to my desired career goal and destination?" If so, consider accepting the opportunity and, if not, consider passing on the opportunity. If not, identify and/or propose an opportunity that addresses a business gap or opportunity and aligns with your career path and destination.

Understand Realities

Other realities in organizations are that your counterparts may have attended the "right" schools and already have strong, supportive, and leverageable networks in place. As a result, they may be better positioned than you for upcoming desirable career opportunities. With that in mind, the OWN IT process can help you neutralize these realities by confirming your strengths, accomplishments, and growth. OWN IT strengthens your self-confidence and self-belief. It fuels your intentionality and proactivity and provides the process and guidance needed to successfully identify, plan, and pursue your desired career destination while effectively developing and leveraging your own trusted advocates.

The OWN IT Process Checklist and Ideas to Remember

Copies of the Personal Balance Sheet and Living Career Action Plan templates are available for your use in the resources section of this book.

"The will to win, the desire to succeed, the urge
to reach your full potential...these are the keys
that will unlock the door to personal excellence."

—CONFUCIUS

Remember, you deserve and owe it to yourself to have and live the career you want! Please remember the following in order to effectively leverage the five-step OWN IT process covered in the previous chapters.

- Confirm your Personal Purpose Statement. Confirm the mantra that gets you up each day and summarizes how you'd like others to know and remember you.

- Prepare and reflect on the results of completing your Personal Balance Sheet. What are your key takeaways that help confirm and support your career direction, goals, and destination?

- Complete the steps of the OWN IT process and embrace positive, proactive, and intentional beliefs and behaviors while identifying the one or two actions you could focus on doing more or differently for each step.

- Review and prioritize your "do-more-of-or-differently" list based on the importance to your career direction, goals, and destination.

- Review and prioritize your key takeaways from your Personal Balance Sheet based on importance to your career direction, goals, and destination.

- After reviewing your Personal Purpose Statement, your "do-more-of-or-differently" list, and your

Personal Balance Sheet takeaways, prepare your initial Living Career Action Plan.

- Review and finalize your draft Living Career Action Plan. Note its alignment with your Personal Purpose, Personal Balance Sheet takeaways, and your "do-more-of-or-differently" list.

- Schedule time to share your Living Career Action Plan. Ideally, you should share this with your Personal Board of Directors (PBOD) and key advocates.

- Regularly schedule time for self-reflection to ensure the effective execution of your Living Career Action Plan.

- Consider revisiting and reflecting on the five steps of the OWN IT process at least annually to note what's changed for you.

- Reflect on and update your Personal Purpose Statement and Personal Balance Sheet at least annually and ensure you're living your purpose and leveraging your assets.

- Review and reflect on your Living Career Action Plan at least annually and, if needed, update your plan and share it with your key advocates, coaches, mentors, and sponsors.

I know the process of proactively and intentionally owning your career seems like a lot of work, and it is. Aren't you worth doing the work necessary to have the career and life you deserve instead of leaving it all to chance?

You have the perpetual opportunity and responsibility to be the captain of your career. You can do it when you make a continuous, intentional, and proactive personal investment in your career. Remember, you have a choice!

The OWN IT process is here to help you confirm your career direction and identify the important steps and relationships necessary to reach your desired career destination. By using the OWN IT process, you benefit from increased self-confidence and self-belief; increased comfort with self-promotion and vulnerability by being more of who you are; and leveraging your growth mindset and continuous learning. By doing this work, you are a role model. You lead the way for both yourself and others. You create positive ripple effects and benefits for team members and the larger organization. You got this.

"The question isn't who's going to let me; it's who is going to stop me."

AYN RAND

Lessons Learned

Sample Key Career Lessons I Learned

Following are key lessons I learned and leveraged in developing and executing my career goals and plan. These lessons included learning the importance of the following:

- **Self-belief and trust** to learn what I needed to be seen as a successful contributing collaborator with others.

- **Continuous learning** to identify and fill my knowledge gaps and expand my capabilities and experiences.

- **Speaking up** and sharing my point of view to be seen as a knowledgeable and collaborative contributor.

- **Learning** from my mistakes, owning them, and letting them go.

- **Being aware** of and understanding organizational politics, who has power, and how decisions are made.

- **Not taking situations personally** and being comfortable controlling what I can and not worrying about the things I can't.

- **Understanding** that having the right advocates (trusted coaches, colleagues, mentors, and sponsors) can lead to increased peace of mind, self-confidence, visibility, and career progression.

- **Letting go of the fear** of rejection and instead growing, leveraging, and sustaining the right relationships in my network for advice, counsel, and sponsorship.

- **Confidently knowing and defining who I am** and what's important rather than looking to others to define me, my value, and future.

How to Use the Next Pages:

On the following pages, you'll see two versions of the Personal Balance Sheet side by side. On the left is Sheila's completed example, showing you the kinds of thoughts and details you might include. On the right is a blank template for you to fill in yourself. This layout is designed so you can easily look at Sheila's example as a reference while you work through your own sheet.

Sheila's Sample Initial Personal Balance Sheet

Objective:

To summarize and consolidate key elements for the development of your Living Career Action Plan.

Instructions:

Reflect and summarize your responses for each of the following topics in the space provided.

1. **Your Purpose**: Who are you? What do you care deeply about? What do you want to accomplish with your life? What do you want your legacy to be—i.e., what others will say about you?

   Establish a legacy of making a difference in the world by building authentic, trusting relationships and helping others by sharing and giving back in both my personal and professional lives.

Template
Initial Personal
Balance Sheet

Objective:

To summarize and consolidate key elements for the development of your Living Career Action Plan.

Instructions:

Reflect and summarize your responses for each of the following topics in the space provided.

1. **Your Purpose**: Who are you? What do you care deeply about? What do you want to accomplish with your life? What do you want your legacy to be—i.e., what others will say about you?

2. **Your Career Vision**: When you think of your career destination today, what do you see for the near-term (1–3 yrs.)? What do you see for the mid-term (3–5 yrs.)? What do you see for the long-term (5–7 yrs.)? What do you see for the longer term (7+ yrs.)?

- **Near-Term:** Successful Strategy & Operations Partner

- **Mid-Term:** Successful Change Mgmt. Practice Ldr.

- **Long-Term:** Successful Regional Change Mgmt. Ldr.

- **Longer Term:** Successful Global Change Mgmt. Managing Partner

3. **Your Values**: What are the top 5 values you live by? How well are your current organization's values aligned with yours?

Authenticity	Empathy
Reliability	Integrity
Trust	

My values of Authenticity, Reliability, Integrity and Trust are aligned and compatible with the organization's; however, there is misalignment between my view of Empathy and my experience of it in the organization.

2. **Your Career Vision**: When you think of your career destination today, what do you see for the near-term (1–3 yrs.)? What do you see for the mid-term (3–5 yrs.)? What do you see for the long-term (5–7 yrs.)? What do you see for the longer term (7+ yrs.)?

3. **Your Values**: What are the top 5 values you live by? How well are your current organization's values aligned with yours?

Your Assets & Opportunities

4. **Your Education**: What formal education, training, and/or personal study have you completed to help you achieve your career goals? What additional education, if any, will you need?

   - BS Accounting
   - MS Change Management
   - MBA Strategic Marketing

5. **Your Career Experiences**: What is your ideal career destination? What roles have you held that helped prepare you for your desired career path and destination? What additional experiences will you need to position you as a strong candidate to move up to the next role along your career path? How will you get these additional experiences?

   - Ideal: Global Change Mgmt. Managing Partner
   - Preparatory Roles: Strategy & Operations (S&O) Partner, S&O Sr. Mgr., S&O Project Mgr.
   - Additional Experiences needed: Change Mgmt. Ldr., Change Mgmt. Partner
   - Get Additional Experiences: Sustain Change Management expertise with additional education/training. Also identify internal and/or external opportunities to apply expertise with help of Mentors and Sponsors

Your Assets & Opportunities

4. **Your Education:** What formal education, training, and/or personal study have you completed to help you achieve your career goals? What additional education, if any, will you need?

5. **Your Career Experiences:** What is your ideal career destination? What roles have you held that helped prepare you for your desired career path and destination? What additional experiences will you need to position you as a strong candidate to move up to the next role along your career path? How will you get these additional experiences?

6. **Your Key Career Accomplishments**: What have been the most defining peaks (joys) and valleys (disappointments) of your career? What did you learn from them? What are your proudest career accomplishments to date? What did they confirm for you?

- **Peaks**: Becoming a Strategy & Operations Partner, consistently meeting/exceeding client expectations, extremely effective with client relationship management.
- **Valleys**: As a female POC, only modest feelings of belonging.
- **Proudest**: Trusted Advisor Status with clients.
- **Confirmed**: I'm an extremely capable and valuable resource for my clients and the firm and both value my contributions.

7. **Your Professional Certifications/Licenses**: What certifications and/or licenses have you earned to date? What others may help you accomplish your career goals?

Licensed CPA   Certified Project Mgr.
Certified Change Mgmt. Professional

6. **Your Key Career Accomplishments**: What have been the most defining peaks (joys) and valleys (disappointments) of your career? What did you learn from them? What are your proudest career accomplishments to date? What did they confirm for you?

7. **Your Professional Certifications/Licenses**: What certifications and/or licenses have you earned to date? What others may help you accomplish your career goals?

8. **Your Key Professional Strengths**: What are your key strengths? Which strengths could you leverage more to make a greater impact and achieve your career goals?

- Servant Leadership
- Strategic/Critical Thinker
- Trusted Advisor
- Client Relationship Mgmt.
- Project Planning, Mgmt. And Execution
- Analytical
- Networking
- Continuous/Fearless Learner

9. **Your Key Career Development Opportunities**: What are your most important development opportunities to convert to strengths to help you achieve your career goals? What will your initial step(s)/action(s) be?

- Explore opportunities to begin expanding regional and global leadership knowledge and skills.
- Explore the process and requirements to become a Regional Managing Partner.
- Explore the process and requirements to become a Global Client Services Partner (GCP).

8. **Your Key Professional Strengths**: What are your key strengths? Which strengths could you leverage more to make a greater impact and achieve your career goals?

9. **Your Key Career Development Opportunities**: What are your most important development opportunities to convert to strengths to help you achieve your career goals? What will your initial step(s)/action(s) be?

10. **Your Key Relationships**: Who are the existing key mentor and sponsor relationships in your network? How might you better nurture, strengthen, and leverage these relationships further to help you achieve your career goals? Who else should you add to your network?

    - Regional S&O Practice Ldr.

    - S&O Markets Ldr.

    - Regional Managing Partner

    - US Markets Ldr.

    - US Managing Partner

11. **Your Professional Attitude**: Your attitude affects your mood, emotions, and ability to contribute the way you'd like. It can also affect others around you. How would you describe your traditional attitude? What, if anything, would you change? Change requires self-awareness and the solicitation of periodic feedback from others.

    - Capable

    - Optimistic

    - Self-Aware

    - Guarded: Feel the need to continually prove myself.

10. **Your Key Relationships**: Who are the existing key mentor and sponsor relationships in your network? How might you better nurture, strengthen, and leverage these relationships further to help you achieve your career goals? Who else should you add to your network?

11. **Your Professional Attitude**: Your attitude affects your mood, emotions, and ability to contribute the way you'd like. It can also affect others around you. How would you describe your traditional attitude? What, if anything, would you change? Change requires self-awareness and the solicitation of periodic feedback from others.

12. **Your Career Energy Management**: During the course of a day, when are you the most energetic? When are you the least energetic? What drains your energy? What replenishes your energy? What can you do to sustain your energy and be your best self?

- **Most**: Morning hours (earlier the better)

- **Least**: Evening hours

- **Drains**: Rework and unproductive meetings

- **Replenish**: Exercise & Mindfulness

- **Sustain**: Self-Reflection and Mindfulness

13. **Your Key Career Wants and Preferences**: Think of a time(s) in life and/or career when things were going really well. What insights/learnings about your wants and preferences can you take from those times? How do these insights inform your wants and preferences today? What are your key wants and preferences now?

- Clear Goals

- Achievable Expectations

- Clear Roles & Responsibilities

- Trusting Mentors & Sponsors

- Clear, Actionable Feedback

- Available Resources

- Respect

- Feelings of Belonging

12. **Your Career Energy Management**: During the course of a day, when are you the most energetic? When are you the least energetic? What drains your energy? What replenishes your energy? What can you do to sustain your energy and be your best self?

13. **Your Key Career Wants and Preferences**: Think of a time(s) in life and/or career when things were going really well. What insights/learnings about your wants and preferences can you take from those times? How do these insights inform your wants and preferences today? What are your key wants and preferences now?

14. **Your Key Career Needs**: What are your essential, key needs for you to have the successful career you want?

   - Supportive Mentors & Sponsors
   - Career Advancement Opportunities
   - Recognition for Contributions
   - Adequate Resources
   - Leadership Commitment
   - Reasonable Expectations

15. **Your Key Career/Life Priorities**: What's important to you in your personal life? What's important to you in your professional life? Are your personal and professional lives in alignment/in sync? If not, what will you do to get them in better alignment?

   - Work/Life Alignment & Self-Care
   - Reasonable, Clear Role and Expectations
   - Feelings of Belonging to Be Myself in Life and at Work
   - Continuous Learning and Growth
   - Calendarize Regular Time for Self-Reflection
   - Expand and Sustain My Network of Mentors/Sponsors

14. **Your Key Career Needs**: What are your essential, key needs for you to have the successful career you want?

15. **Your Key Career/Life Priorities**: What's important to you in your personal life? What's important to you in your professional life? Are your personal and professional lives in alignment/in sync? If not, what will you do to get them in better alignment?

16. **Your Key Career Goals**: What are your key career goals for the near-term (1–3 yrs.), mid-term (3–5 yrs.), long-term (5–7 yrs.), and longer term (7+ yrs.)?

   - **Near-Term:** Become Trusted Advisor among S&O clients

   - **Mid-Term:** Develop Industry Reputation among clients in Change Mgmt. Consulting

   - **Long-Term:** Develop a Regional & National Reputation among clients in Change Mgmt. Leadership & Consulting

   - **Longer Term:** Be seen as Global Resource for Global Change Mgmt. across the Firm and among Global clients

17. **Your Key Actions Needed to Achieve Your Career Goals**: What are the 1–3 key actions you will take to achieve your near-term goals? What are the 1–3 key actions you will take to achieve your mid-term goals? What are the 1–3 actions you will take to achieve your long-term goals? What are the 1-3 actions you will take to achieve your longer-term goals?

   1. Confirm my level of interest in becoming a Change Mgmt. Practice Ldr.

   2. Present my Business Case for becoming Change Mgmt. Practice Ldr. to key decision-makers at the firm.

   3. Get advice and counsel and support from my Personal Board of Directors (selected mentors and sponsors) for becoming a Change Mgmt. Practice Ldr.

16. **Your Key Career Goals**: What are your key career goals for the near-term (1–3 yrs.), mid-term (3–5 yrs.), long-term (5–7 yrs.), and longer term (7+ yrs.)?

17. **Your Key Actions Needed to Achieve Your Career Goals**: What are the 1–3 key actions you will take to achieve your near-term goals? What are the 1–3 key actions you will take to achieve your mid-term goals? What are the 1–3 actions you will take to achieve your long-term goals? What are the 1-3 actions you will take to achieve your longer-term goals?

4. Continually grow my knowledge/skills by seeking and successfully leading challenging Change Mgmt. client work Regionally, Nationally and Globally

18. **Your Key Measures**: What criteria will you use to measure your career success for the near-term, the mid-term, and the long-term?

- **Near-Term:** Development and Execution of an Action Plan

- **Mid-Term:** Approval of Business Case and approval to assume the role of Change Mgmt. Practice Ldr. by firm's decision-makers

- **Long-Term:** Expanded positive Regional, National, and Global reputation, positive Client feedback and Favorable Business Results

- **Longer-Term:** Significant Global Leadership role with the Firm and Global Change Mgmt. Recognition outside the Firm.

18. **Your Key Measures**: What criteria will you use to measure your career success for the near-term, the mid-term, and the long-term?

19. **Your Passion and Commitment to Career Self-Management**: How passionate and committed are you to achieve your career goals? What might you do more of or differently to raise your passion and commitment levels? What will you do to sustain your level of passion and commitment to achieve your goals?

- I have high Passion and believe it's achievable
- Continued self-reflection, accomplishments, learnings, opportunities, and challenges
- Continue to solicit input from mentors & sponsors
- Plan, act, solicit feedback, learn and course correct
- Manage my Energy
- Commit to Work/Life alignment and self-care

19. **Your Passion and Commitment to Career Self-Management**: How passionate and committed are you to achieve your career goals? What might you do more of or differently to raise your passion and commitment levels? What will you do to sustain your level of passion and commitment to achieve your goals?

20. **Your Key Resources for Career Support**: Who are the key trusted advocates, including colleagues, coaches, mentors, and sponsors, in your network? Who should you add to your network of advocates? Of your mentors and sponsors, who should you identify as members of your Personal Board of Directors?

- Sustain key Personal Board of Directors (PBOD) mentors/sponsors

- Reciprocate the support of Personal BOD members by helping them with priorities

- Expand and sustain mentors and sponsors

- Continue to share and receive input on career goals and action plans from coaches, mentors, and sponsors

20. **Your Key Resources for Career Support**: Who are the key trusted advocates, including colleagues, coaches, mentors, and sponsors, in your network? Who should you add to your network of advocates? Of your mentors and sponsors, who should you identify as members of your Personal Board of Directors?

21. **Your Key Career Challenges**: What are the key near-term, mid-term, and long-term challenges you will face to achieve your career goals? What actions must you be prepared to take to successfully navigate these challenges?

- Proactively asking for help, feedback, advice, and counsel from mentors and sponsors
- Giving myself permission to put myself and interests first
- Executing work/life boundaries and self-care
- Giving myself grace when things don't go as planned
- Schedule and sustain regular time for self-reflection
- Being a lifelong, continuous learner who learns from mistakes
- Thinking beyond job titles when engaged in career planning

22. **Your Celebrations**: How will you celebrate your career successes? With whom do you want to celebrate your successes?

- Frequent family outings acknowledging their support
- Quarterly individual and team recognition celebrations of success
- Regular acknowledgment of mentor and sponsor support

INITIAL PERSONAL BALANCE SHEET · TEMPLATE

21. **Your Key Career Challenges**: What are the key near-term, mid-term, and long-term challenges you will face to achieve your career goals? What actions must you be prepared to take to successfully navigate these challenges?

22. **Your Celebrations**: How will you celebrate your career successes? With whom do you want to celebrate your successes?

23. **Your Key Timeline:** When will you prepare, implement, and begin executing your Living Career Action Plan? What key milestones will you establish to keep you on track?

- Within 90 days: Develop Initial Living Career Action Plan, Business Case and Business Plan

- Within 120 days: Get input from Mentors/Sponsors on Career Plan, Business Case, and Business Plan

- Within 180 days: Launch Career Plan and present Business Case and Business Plan to Key Decision-Makers

- Within 200 days: Launch approved Business Case and Business Plan

- Review Living Career Action Plan Progress at least annually and make course corrections as needed

- Review Business Plan Progress Quarterly and make course corrections as needed

- Continue to solicit frequent input from coaches, mentors, and sponsors on both Career Plan and Business Plan progress

23. **Your Key Timeline**: When will you prepare, implement, and begin executing your Living Career Action Plan? What key milestones will you establish to keep you on track?

Notes

Notes

How to Use the Next Pages:

On the following pages, you'll see two versions of the Living Career Action Plan side by side. On the left is Sheila's completed example, showing you the kinds of thoughts and details you might include. On the right is a blank template for you to fill in yourself. This layout is designed so you can easily look at Sheila's example as a reference while you work through your own plan.

Sheila's Sample Initial Living Career Action Plan

Key Goals/Opportunities:

1. **What do I need to address to have the career I want?**

   - Confirm Change Mgmt. Practice Ldr as preferred career direction.

   - Identify key decision-makers for Change Mgmt. Practice Ldr role.

   - Identify/expand network of key mentors and sponsors.

Key Actions:

2. **What key actions am I prepared to take?**

   - Confirm alignment with purpose, passions, strengths, and next steps. Calendarize regular time for reflection.

   - Present business case for Change Mgmt. Practice Ldr with decision-makers. Schedule regular reflection time.

   - Identify Personal Board of Directors (BOD) for support of Living Career Action Plan. Schedule regular reflection time.

Template
Initial Living Career
Action Plan

Key Goals/Opportunities:

1. **What do I need to address to have the career I want?**

Key Actions:

2. **What key actions am I prepared to take?**

Key Resources:

3. **Mentors and sponsors I will need? Other needs?**

    - Get and act on advice and counsel of BOD, mentors, and sponsors.

Challenges:

4. **What key challenges will I face? How will I navigate them?**

    - Give myself permission to reflect and act. Calendarize regular self-reflection.

    - Make a compelling business case for Change Mgmt. Practice Ldr.

    - Develop reciprocal vs. transactional relationships with BOD members.

Key Resources:

3. **Mentors and sponsors I will need? Other needs?**

Challenges:

4. **What key challenges will I face? How will I navigate them?**

Measures:

5. **What will success look like? How will I measure success?**

   - Successful implementation of clear, actionable action plan.
   - Endorsement of business case and appointed Change Mgmt. Practice Ldr.
   - Execute effective, reciprocal relationships with my BOD.

Timing:

6. **When will I start? What will be my key milestones?**

   - Q1: Develop and implement action plan. Quarterly reflect on progress and course correct.
   - Q1/2: Present and Implement business case. Quarterly monitor success in role and course correct.
   - Q1: Invite select network members to serve on Personal BOD. Quarterly reflect on progress and reciprocity.

Measures:

5. **What will success look like? How will I measure success?**

Timing:

6. **When will I start? What will be my key milestones?**

Notes

Notes

Works Cited

Dweck, Carol S. 2006. *Mindset: The New Psychology of Success.* Random House.

Dweck, Carol S. 2014. "The Power of Believing You Can Improve." Norrköping, Sweden. September 2014. TED video, 10:22. https://www.youtube.com/watch?v=_XomgOOSpLU.

FranklinCovey. 2021. "The 13 Behaviours of High Trust." October 11, 2021. https://www.franklincovey.co.uk/blog/2021/10/11/the-13-behaviours-of-high-trust/

Garvey Berger, J. 2020. *Unlocking Leadership Mindtraps: How to Thrive in Complexity.* Stanford University Press.

Leider, Richard J. 2015. *The Power of Purpose: Find Meaning, Live Longer, Better.* Berrett-Koehler Publishers.

Matthews, Gail. 2007. "The Impact of Commitment, Accountability, and Written Goals on Goal Achievement." Psychology | Faculty Presentations. https://scholar.dominican.edu/psychology-faculty-conference-presentations/3

Maxwell, John C. 2007. *Failing Forward: Turning Mistakes into Stepping Stones for Success.* Harper Collins Leadership.

Philbin, John. 2018. "The Four Types of Networkers." Happy Spectacular (blog), Happy Spectacular website, January 11, 2018. https://happyspectacular.com/2018/01/the-four-types-of-networkers/.

Schein, Edgar. 2013. *Humble Inquiry: The Gentle Art of Asking Instead of Telling.* Berrett-Koehler Publishers.

Schelleger, Vern. 2023. "What are the Eight Networking Competencies?" 40Plus of Greater Washington presentation available on YouTube. December 3, 2023. Video, 5:25. https://www.youtube.com/watch?v=bo8BxLIQn8A.

Wells, Rachel. 2023. "5 Types of People You Need in Your Network to Build Leadership Skills." Forbes. December 3, 2023. https://www.forbes.com/sites/rachelwells/2023/12/03/5-types-of-people-you-need-in-your-network-to-build-leadership-skills/

About the Author

Hi, I'm Robert Corbett! I help build better leaders faster by partnering with them to identify the clarity they need when they need it most!

I'm a Professional Certified Coach (PCC) with the Hudson Institute of Coaching and the International Coach Federation (ICF). My specialties include Leadership, Inclusion, and Retirement coaching. I'm also certified in several assessment tools including Leadership Circle Profile, Immunity to Change, Hogan Assessment, COMMTT Inclusive Behavior Framework, and Myers-Briggs.

I help clients meet or exceed their personal and organizational goals by leveraging their strengths, addressing their learning/development opportunities, strengthening the alignment and trust between them and their teams.

I believe coaching clients are whole and fully capable of identifying their best paths forward including their Purpose, Vision, Goals and Action Plan. As a coach, I partner with them to help identify the specific and relevant actions, challenges, success factors/metrics and timelines to successfully execute their plans. We also partner to identify the key supportive resources (i.e., trusted advisors including coaches, colleagues, mentors and sponsors) needed for success. We also discuss the importance of self-reflection and intentionality to effectively allocate their energy and time.

I have 20+ years of experience in leadership, coaching and consulting roles. I've led cross-functional teams and worked in 10+ countries in industries including manufacturing, technology, aerospace, healthcare, financial services, energy, education, business services and government.

A representative list of organizations where I've served in Coaching, Human Resources leadership or consultative roles includes EY, Kraft Foods, PWC, the AHA, Exelon, Baxter Healthcare, TRW, Levi Strauss & Co., and The Hay Group.

Thank You for Reading My Book!

I hope you've found it to be insightful and helpful.

Please visit my website at www.fullyaligned.com to view our service offerings, contact us and/or download the templates referenced in the book:

- Personal Balance Sheet
- Living Career Action Plan

Leave a Review!

For a self-published author like myself, reviews mean the world! So please, leave an honest review on the platform from which you purchased this book. I read every one! Thank you.

www.ingramcontent.com/pod-product-compliance
Lightning Source LLC
Chambersburg PA
CBHW040923210326
41597CB00030B/5154